Discover the
Southern Adirondacks

Walks, Waterways, and Winter Treks

Discover the Southern Adirondacks

Walks, Waterways, and Winter Treks

Barbara McMartin

with the assistance of Stanford Pulrang
Photographs by Lawrence King and Barbara McMartin

Backcountry Publications
Woodstock, Vermont

An Invitation to the Reader

Over time trails can be rerouted and signs and landmarks altered. If you find that changes have occurred on the routes described in this book, please let us know so that corrections may be made in future editions. The author and publisher also welcome other comments and suggestions. Address all correspondence to:

Editor
Discover the Adirondacks Series
Backcountry Publications
P.O. Box 175
Woodstock, VT 05091

Library of Congress Cataloging-in-Publication Data

McMartin, Barbara.
  Discover the southern Adirondacks: walks, waterways, and winter treks / Barbara McMartin with the assistance of Stanford Pulrang.
  p. cm. — (Discover the Adirondacks series : 6)
  Rev. ed. of: Discover the Adirondacks / Barbara McMartin. ©1979–
  Bibliography: p.
  Includes index.
  ISBN 0-942440-41-2 (pbk.)
  1. Outdoor recreation—New York (State)—Adirondack Mountains—Guide-books. 2. Hiking—New York (State)—Adirondack Mountains—Guide-books. 3. Winter sports—New York (State)—Adirondack Mountains—Guide-books. 4. Adirondack Mountains (N.Y.)—Description and travel—Guide-books. I. Pulrang, Stanford. II. McMartin, Barbara. Discover the Adirondacks. III. Title. IV. Series.
  GV191.42.N7M37   1988
  917.47′53—dc19   87-34917
                                                                CIP

Published by Backcountry Publications, Inc.
Woodstock, Vermont 05091

Printed in the United States of America by McNaughton & Gunn
Typesetting by the Sant Bani Press
Series design by Leslie Fry
Layout by Barbara McMartin
Maps by Richard Widhu

Photograph credits
Lawrence King, 6, 63, 65, 81, 98, 102, 119, 122, 130, 149, 175, 178
Barbara McMartin, 18, 28, 33, 39, 42, 60, 85, 104, 107, 136, 145, 170
W. Alec Reid, 2, 49, 56, 75, 96

Photographs
Cover: *Winter lights near Canada Lake (Lawrence King)*
Page 2: *Along the Northville-Placid Trail south of Piseco*
Page 6: *Balancing Rock on the way to Sherman Mountain*

Acknowledgements

This is the third revision of my first guide, *Walks and Waterways*. Among the many people who discovered the region by using earlier editions was Stanford Pulrang who settled in the Canada Lake area in 1982. Since then he has walked almost all the trails in this guide, commented extensively on their descriptions, and found a number of new, challenging, and rewarding bushwhacks. He has been out almost every day in some part of the area. Best of all, he has been a delightful companion when I have revisited well-loved places. This revision owes much to his careful checking of so many routes.

Howard and Anna Ulman also moved to the area. They built a home in Benson and have rechecked a number of trails and bushwhacks in the eastern part of the guide.

Larry and Maryde King continue to snowshoe the very snowy mountains in southern Hamilton County, and we have enjoyed revisiting these places in their company.

Francis B. Rosevear and his wife, Ruth, have spent several visits exploring the Brayhouse Gore and the location of the wandering survey point, which Francis has described for this guide.

Forest Ranger John Seifts suggested the climb on Rogers Mountain.

My husband, W. Alec Reid, produces the fine black and white prints used in this series, and he has hiked and skied many of the local trails with me.

Willard Reed revisited some of the bushwhacks, the ones he introduced me to for the second edition.

Because the area covered by the guide is so close to our summer home, all my children have enjoyed walks there. The comments on trail descriptions from my son, James McMartin Long, are especially welcome.

We all spend so much time in these woods and on these streams that it is more fun than work keeping the guidebook up-to-date. Fun or no, the efforts of all who helped are much appreciated.

Contents

Introduction

THE SILVER LAKE Wilderness is the third largest Wilderness Area in the Adirondack Park. It is traversed from north to south by the Northville-Placid Trail. The rest is almost without marked trails. There are only a few sportsmen's paths, so the region remains as little known and used as any part of the Forest Preserve. The Shaker Mountain Wild Forest to the south and the Ferris Lake Wild Forest to the west have numerous snowmobile trails and many sportsmen's paths.

The shortage of routes for the hiker, snowshoer, or cross-country skier is only real for those who lack a sense of adventure; for if you want to discover unusual places, all fairly easy to get to, this is the area for you. The trails in the Wild Forest Areas are well-marked for the hiker and generally well-maintained.

There are as many quiet lakes and streams or fields of wildflowers and places to bird as in any part of the Adirondacks; and there are far fewer people. This solitary paradise is a little better known than when I first wrote about it in 1974, but it still holds some of the least used areas of the Adirondacks.

It seems incongruous that an area only 20 miles from the Mohawk Valley and so near large centers of population can remain so little used. History explains in part the region's slow growth as a center of recreation.

Because of the proximity to the Mohawk Valley, the forests were easily harvested for lumber and tanbark. When the forests were depleted in the decades around the turn of the century, huge blocks of land were acquired by the state, leaving little for private development.

The railroad north from Utica to Old Forge and on to Blue Mountain Lake and Raquette Lake opened the forests to the west to eager vacationers in the second half of the nineteenth century. Lakes George and Champlain and later the overland routes in their valleys brought people to the eastern Adirondacks and provided access to the spectacular High Peaks. The southern areas, covered by this guide, still have few roads.

The principal access, NY 10, also bisects the region. The road follows an old Indian trail and the course laid out in the early nineteenth century by surveyors, who were accompanied by Nick Stoner, a famous trapper. Until the 1960s, this route into the wilderness remained poorly paved and little used. As a result, many of the interior paths that branch from it are less well traveled now than when the area was logged.

A road from yesterday roughly delineates the western boundary of the area covered in this guide. Following the valley of the East Canada Creek, the Powley-Piseco Road stretches from Stratford to NY 10, near Piseco; and much of it is still rough and unpaved. NY 30, which runs through the Sacandaga Valley is the eastern boundary. The Blue Line is the southern boundary and NY 8 is the northern boundary.

In this six-hundred-square-mile area, there are nearly a hundred small uninhabited lakes and ponds. With less than 1500-foot change in elevation, there are few spectacular mountains; nevertheless there are several exciting peaks, almost all reached only by bushwhacks.

Among the many shallow ponds and lakes, there are a few typical quaking bogs. Because most paths follow rivers or streams through valleys, they are, to their detriment, often wet. Leisurely canoe trips make it easy to explore the valleys of two of the rivers that meander through broad flood plains.

A majority of the guide's level trails serve as wilderness ski-touring routes. Cross-country skiing to the myriad lakes east of NY 10 is the best in the Adirondacks. There are deep snows, just enough snowmobile use to pack the trails, but not enough to affect the skier. The few mountains with clifftop views require only gentle climbs and are most easily reached on winter snowshoe treks.

If you love the woods, you will find here many kinds of natural delights, lakes, streams, and waterfalls. Instead of dramatic climbs, you will find paths leading to quiet places to explore and sites of rare beauty along the waterways. A few paths wind into deep woods with no destinations at all. These are good nature walks, strolls from which to enjoy beauty in microcosm.

How to Use the "Discover" Guides

The regional guides in the *Discover the Adirondacks* series will tell you enough about each area so that you can enjoy it in many different ways at any time of year. Each guide will acquaint you with that region's access roads and trailheads, its trails and unmarked paths, some bushwhack routes and canoe trips, and its best picnic spots, campsites, and ski-touring routes. At the same time, the guides will introduce you to valleys, mountains, cliffs, scenic views, lakes, streams, and a myriad of other natural features.

Some of the destinations are within walking distance of the major highways that ring the areas, while others are miles deep into the wilderness. Each description will enable you to determine the best excursion for you and to enjoy the natural features you will pass, whether you are on a summer day hike or a winter ski-touring trek. The sections are grouped in chapters according to their access points. Each chapter contains a brief introduction to that area's history and the old settlements and industries that have all but disappeared into wilderness. Throughout the guides you will find accounts of the geological forces that shaped features of the land. Unusual wildflowers and forest stands also will be noted.

It is our hope that you will find this guide not only an invitation to know and enjoy the woods but a companion for all your adventures there.

MAPS AND NOMENCLATURE

The Adirondack Atlas, a map published by City Street Directory of Poughkeepsie, New York, is the best reference for town roads, and it has the added advantage of identifying state land. In spite of the fact that it has not been updated to show recent acquisitions, this is a valuable aid in the southern region where public and private lands are so intricately mixed.

This guide contains maps that show all the routes mentioned and the maps are adequate for the marked trails. You may still want to carry the USGS topographic quadrangle sheets for the region, and you ought to have them for the more difficult bushwhacks. The maps used include 7.5-minute series Canada Lake, Caroga Lake, Stratford, Lassellsville, Jackson Summit, and Northville; and the 15-minute series for Piseco and Lake Pleasant.

The 15-minute maps are reproduced in the same scale, 1" = 1 mile. The 7.5-minute maps are uniformly reduced by 62 percent. *Note carefully this change in scale.* The scale is given on the reproduced maps and this percentage was chosen to give the greatest possible details as well as coverage.

Maps are available locally in many sporting goods stores. The Canada Lake Store stocks all local maps. You can order maps from USGS Map Distribution Branch, Box 25286, Denver Federal Center, Denver, CO 80225. Maps are currently more easily obtained from a private source, Timely Discount Topos. You can call them at 1-800-821-7609; with your credit card number they will ship maps within a week.

The guide uses the spelling given in the USGS but local variations are noted.

DISTANCE AND TIME

Distance along the routes is measured from the USGS survey maps and is accurate to within 10 percent. Few hikers gauge distance accurately even on well-defined trails. Distance is a variable factor in comparing routes along trails, paths, or bushwhacks. Because the new maps are just as easily read in miles as meters, this guide continues to give distance in the more familiar miles. However, the metric maps give elevation in 10-meter contours, so elevation is given in both meters and feet.

Time is given as an additional gauge for the length of routes. This provides a better understanding of the difficulty of the terrain, the change of elevation, and the problems of finding a suitable course. Average time for walking trails is 2 miles an hour, 3 miles if the way is level and well defined; for paths, 1½ to 2 miles an hour; and for bushwhacks, 1 mile an hour.

Summaries for distance, time, and vertical rise are given with the title of each section describing a trail or path. These distances and times are for *one way only*, unless otherwise stated.

TYPES OF ROUTES

Each section of this guide generally describes a route or a place. Included in the descriptions are such basic information as the suitability for different levels of woods experience, walking (or skiing, paddling, and climbing) times, distances, directions to the access, and, of course, directions along the route itself. The following definitions clarify the terms used in this book.

A route is considered a *trail* if it is so designated by the New York State Department of Environmental Conservation (DEC). This means the trail is routinely cleared by DEC or volunteer groups and adequately marked with official DEC disks. *Blue disks* generally indicate major north-south routes, *red disks* indicate east-west routes, and *yellow disks* indicate side trails. This scheme is not, however, applied consistently throughout the Adirondacks.

Some trails have been marked for *cross-country skiing*, and new *pale yellow disks with a skier* are used. *Large orange disks* indicate *snowmobile trails*, which are limited to some portions of Wild Forest Areas. Snowmobiles are permitted on them in winter when there is sufficient snow cover. Many snowmobile trails on the interior are not heavily used and can be shared by those on cross-country skis as long as the skier is cautious. Hikers can enjoy both ski and snowmobile trails.

A *path* is an informal and unmarked route with a clearly defined foot tread. These traditional routes, worn by fishermen and hunters to favorite spots, are great for hiking. A path, however, is not necessarily kept open, and fallen trees and new growth sometimes obliterate its course. The paths that cross wet meadows or open fields often become concealed by lush growth. You should always carry a map and compass when you are following an unmarked path and you should keep track of your location.

There is a safe prescription for walking paths. In a group of three or more hikers, stringing out along a narrow path will permit the leader to scout until the path disappears, at which point at least one member of the party should still be standing on an obvious part of the path. If that hiker remains standing while those in front range out to find the path, the whole group can continue safely after a matter of moments.

Hikers in the north country often use the term *bushwhack* to describe an uncharted and unmarked trip. Sometimes bushwhacking literally means pushing brush aside, but it usually connotes a variety of cross-country walks.

Bushwhacks are an important part of this regional guide series because of the shortage of marked trails throughout much of the Adirondack Park and the abundance of little-known and highly desirable destinations for which no visible routes exist. Although experienced bushwhackers may reach these destinations with not much more help than the knowledge of their location, I think most hikers will appreciate these simple descriptions that point out the easiest and most interesting routes and the possible pitfalls. In general, descriptions for bushwhacks are less detailed than those for paths or trails; it is assumed that those who bushwhack have a greater knowledge of the woods than those who walk marked routes.

Bushwhack is defined as any trip on which you make your way through the woods without a trail, path, or the visible foot tread of other hikers and without markings, signs, or blazes. It also means you will make your way by following a route chosen on a contour map, aided by a compass, using streambeds, valleys, abandoned roads, and obvious ridges as guides. Most bushwhacks require navigating by both contour map and compass, and an understanding of the terrain.

Bushwhack distances are not given in precise tenths of a mile. They are estimates representing the shortest distance one could travel between points. This reinforces the fact that each hiker's cross-country route will be different, yielding different mileages.

A bushwhack is said to be *easy* if the route is along a stream, a lakeshore, a reasonably obvious abandoned roadway, or some similarly well-defined feature. A short route to the summit of a hill or a small mountain can often be easy. A bushwhack is termed *moderate* if a simple route can be defined on a contour map and followed with the aid of a compass. Previous experience is necessary. A bushwhack is rated *difficult* if it entails a complex route, necessitating advanced knowledge of navigation by compass and reading contour maps and land features.

Compass directions for bushwhacks are given in degrees from magnetic north, a phrase abbreviated here to *degrees magnetic*.

The guide occasionally refers to old *blazed* lines or trails. The word "blaze" comes from the French *blesser* and means to cut or wound. Early loggers and settlers made deep slashes in good-sized trees with an axe to mark property lines and trails. Later, hunters and fishermen often made slashes with knives and, though they are not as deep as axe cuts, they too can still be seen. Following an old blazed path for miles in dense woods is often a challenging but good way to reach a trailless destination. Remember, though, that it is now, and has been for many years, illegal to deface trees in the Forest Preserve in this manner.

You may see *yellow paint daubs on a line of trees.* These lines usually indicate the boundary between private and public lands. Individuals have also used different colors of paint to mark informal routes from time to time. Although it is not legal to mark trails on state land, this guide does refer to such informally marked paths.

All *vehicular traffic,* except snowmobiles on their designated trails, is *prohibited* in the Forest Preserve. Vehicles are allowed on town roads and some roads that pass through state land to reach private inholdings. These roads are described in the guides, and soon the DEC will start marking those old roads that are open to vehicles. Most old roads referred to in the guides are town or logging roads that were abandoned when the land around them became part of the Forest Preserve. Now they are routes for hikers, not for vehicles.

There has been an increase in the use of three- and four-wheeled off-road vehicles, even on trails where such use is prohibited. New laws have gone a long way toward stopping this in the Forest Preserve, ensuring that some of the old roads remain attractive hiking routes.

Cables have been placed across many streams by hunters and other sportsmen to help them cross in high water. The legality of this practice has been challenged. Some may be quite safe to use, others are certainly questionable. Using them is not a recommended practice, so when this guide mentions crossing streams to reach some of the hikes, you are urged to do so only when a boat can be used or in low water when you can wade across.

The *beginning of each section describing a trail* gives a summary of the distance, time, and elevation change for the trail. For unmarked routes, such information is given only within the text of each section—partly to allow for the great variations in the way hikers approach an unmarked route, and partly to emphasize the difficulty of those routes.

PROTECTING THE LAND

Most of the land described in these guides is in the *Forest Preserve,* land set aside a century ago. No trees may be cut on this state land. All of it is open to the public. The *Adirondack Park Agency* has responsibility for the Wilderness, Primitive, and Wild Forest guidelines that govern use of the Forest Preserve. Care and custody of these state lands is left to the Department of Environmental Conservation, which is in the process of producing Unit Management Plans for the roughly 130 separate Forest Preserve areas.

Camping is permitted throughout the public lands except at elevations above 4000 feet and within 150 feet of water or 100 feet of trails. In certain fragile areas, camping is restricted to specific locations, and the state is using a new No Camping disk to mark fragile spots. *Permits* for camping on state lands are needed only for stays that exceed three days or for groups of more than ten campers. Permits can be obtained from the local rangers, who are listed in the area phone books under New York State Department of Environmental Conservation.

Only dead and downed wood can be used for *campfires*. Build fires only when absolutely necessary; carry a small stove for cooking. Build fires at designated fire rings or on rocks or gravelly soil. Fire is dangerous and can travel rapidly through the duff or organic soil, burning roots and spreading through the forest. Douse fires with water, and be sure they are completely out and cold before you leave.

Private lands are generally not open to the public, though some individuals have granted public access across their land to state land. It is always wise to ask before crossing private lands. Be very respectful of private landowners so that public access will continue to be granted. Never enter private lands that have been posted unless you have the owner's permission. Unless the text expressly identifies an area as state-owned Forest Preserve or private land whose owner permits unrestricted public passage, the inclusion of a walk description in this guide does not imply public right-of-way.

Burn combustible trash and carry out everything else.

Most *wildflowers and ferns* mentioned in the text are protected by law. Do not pick them or try to transplant them.

SAFETY IN THE WOODS

It is best *not to walk alone*. Make sure someone knows where you are heading and when you are expected back.

Carry water or other liquids with you. Not only are the mountains dry, but the recent spread of *Giardia* makes many streams suspect. I have an aluminum fuel bottle especially for carrying water; it is virtually indestructible and has a deep screw that prevents leaking.

Carry a small *day pack* with insect repellent, flashlight, first aid kit, emergency food rations, waterproof matches, jackknife, whistle, rain gear, and a wool sweater, even for summer hiking. Wear layers of wool and waterproof clothing in winter and carry an extra sweater and socks. If you plan to camp, consult a good outfitter or a camping organization for the essen-

On Three Ponds Mountain

tials. Better yet, make your first few trips with an experienced leader or with a group.

Always carry a *map and compass*. You may also want to carry an altimeter to judge your progress on bushwhack climbs.

Wear *glasses* when bushwhacking. The risk to your eyes of a small protruding branch makes this a necessity.

Carry *binoculars* for birding as well as for viewing distant peaks.

Use great care near the *edges of cliffs* and when *crossing streams* by hopping rocks in the streambed. Never bushwhack unless you have gained a measure of woods experience. If you are a novice in the out-of-doors, join a hiking group or hire the services of one of the many outfitters in the north country. As you get to know the land, you can progress from the standard trails to the more difficult and more satisfyingly remote routes. Then you will really begin to discover the Adirondacks.

The Powley-Piseco Road

THE POWLEY-PISECO ROAD is a narrow dirt and gravel road for more than half its distance. Because it gives access to so many remote lakes and streams, it is a true wilderness passageway. It intersects NY 10 in the north 0.3 mile south of the bridge over the Big Bay of Piseco Lake. The hamlet of Stratford and 29A are at the southern end of the road 8.6 miles west of NY 10 at Pine Lake. Along the entire nineteen miles in between, you can find the entrances to more walks and adventures than the road has miles.

Signs at the north end call this the Powley Road, after John C. Powley who tried to farm near the headwaters of the East Canada Creek some time before 1880. He left by 1892 and his farm became a boarding house for hunters and fishermen. All that remains is a large clearing.

At the southern end, signs designate it as the Piseco Road, but for descriptive and romantic reasons, I prefer to use the double name. It is not known exactly when in the nineteenth century the road was first used. It may date from before 1850. Even its twentieth century history is vague. A few adventurous travelers remember driving along it in the late 1920s and early 1930s. The bridge over Brayhouse Brook, about a mile south of the half-way point, was washed out in the early 1940s, and the road was not open to cars throughout the rest of the 1940s and into the 1950s.

This romantic wilderness route remains so little known that it is amusing to contemplate the fate it almost suffered. In 1837, a survey was proposed for a railroad between Little Falls and Rackett (Raquette) Lake to run along the East Canada Creek, then north to Piseco's North Shore Road, and then farther north into the wilderness. It was one of the fantasies spun out from Albany to enhance the value of wilderness lands. Fortunately, the level route, almost the same as the Powley-Piseco Road, was never developed.

It was not until the 1970s that the northern dirt portion of the road was widened to accommodate two cars. For a time the opening of the canopy of trees above the road was disturbing, but inexorably the forest is recovering and is closing in, so the trip through the wooded archway is once again a beautiful drive for those who no longer walk. It is still possible to park almost anywhere along the road and enjoy a short walk and rarely be disturbed by the passage of another car. Bordered by mosses and ferns, it offers a reasonably dry place to tramp when other woods trails are too wet for hiking. One of the prettiest sections is the valley between East Notch and West Notch Mountains.

There are several attractive picnic spots along the road or near it, many of which are used by campers. If you drive along the road you will see many turnouts where campers, who do not like to stray too far from their cars, have pulled off to camp, legally, for up to three days without a permit. Some of these sites are within a short distance of the East Canada Creek. Among the picnic spots beside the East Canada, a few are so special as to rival any in the Adirondacks. It is remarkable how secluded you can feel in these quiet nooks and how obvious it is that the unpaved road is responsible for it.

Almost all of the northern two-thirds of the road is in the Forest Preserve; the one big exception is the area called Oregon, where there used to be a dam on the East Canada Creek. The unpaved part of the road, from Oregon to NY 10, is not plowed in winter; snowmobilers use it and many of the trails radiating from it. Therefore, consider the trails in the north as destinations for spring, summer, and fall outings.

You should pay particular attention to directions for the paths north of the confluence of Brayhouse Brook and the East Canada: almost none of them are marked, and the sportsmen who use them are careful to keep the beginnings of some of them concealed. The list of road distances should help, but odometers seem to vary. There have been times when I have had to walk along the road searching for a beginning that I knew was there but remained hidden.

The road traverses a rather flat upland plateau with many shallow lakes and easy, though often wet, paths. In spite of the relatively flat terrain, the area contains some of the most beautiful places covered in this guide.

Several rift valleys, which lie in a northwest to southeast direction, border the road, and one, near Clockmill Corners, is especially lovely. The valleys developed through erosion in the ancient pre-Cambrian rock base, following the fault lines in that basic metamorphic rock.

The large grassy meadows and sand flats at Powley Place, south of Clockmill Corners, are evidence of the glacial lake that covered all of that area. As the lake receded, glacial sand deposits filled the valley. Later the upper reaches of the East Canada Creek cut through the flats, giving the upper portion of that stream its softly eroded banks.

There is relatively little difference in elevation between many of the lakes that drain to form the East Canada, and most unusual is the fact that in recent times several have had their outlet directions change. One, Ferris Lake, has two different outlets, both of which eventually make their way to the East Canada Creek.

Mileages along the Powley-Piseco Road
from South to North

Miles	Section	Place
0.0		Stratford; NY 29A and the Piseco Road, just east of the bridge over the East Canada Creek
0.15		Intersects with Mike Smith Road
0.35		Bridge over Ayres Creek
1.1		Dugway Road left, Red Schoolhouse Road on right
2.2		Fisherman's path west to East Canada Creek
2.5	**1,2**	Hawes Road left, west, to Mussey Dam and iron bridge over East Canada Creek
3.0		Snowmobile trail east to Seeley Road
3.8		Beaver meadow, birding stop
4.35		Seeley Road comes in from east
4.55		New Bridge over North Creek
6.35		Bridge at Oregon, pavement ends, trail to Edick Road, *Discover Southwestern*
6.95	**3**	Path west to House Pond
7.25		Roadside campsite, Oregon
7.5, 7.6		Picnic or campsites
7.75		Picnic site on East Canada Creek, small falls upstream
8.05	**4**	Brayhouse Gore
8.2	**5**	Brayhouse Brook and Potholers
9.65	**6**	Path to Brayhouse Brook, turnout on right, path concealed 150 feet north, just beyond culvert
10.65		Roadside campsites, also at 11.1 and 11.3
10.9	**7-9**	Powley Place Bridge over East Canada Creek
11.35	**10**	Ferris Lake Road
12.45	**11**	Path to Goldmine Stream concealed on west, small, wet, grassy area on right
14.2	**12**	Intermittent stream and path to Christian Lake
14.65		Sandpit on east, right
14.8	**13-17**	Clockmill Corners—trail right 5 miles to Kennels Pond, 6 miles to Averys; trail on left 100 feet north to Evergreen Lake
15.4	**18**	Mud Pond path on right; snowmobile trail 100 yards north on left
16.15	**19**	Camping spot
16.95	**20**	Sand Lake
19.1		NY 10

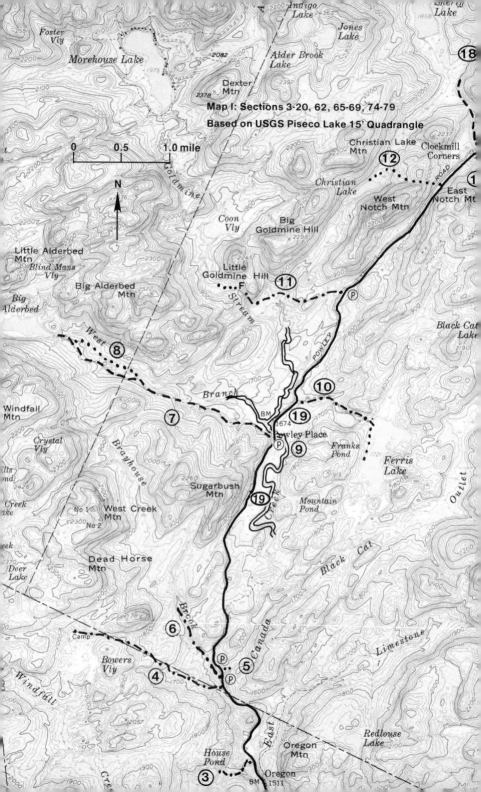

Map I: Sections 3-20, 62, 65-69, 74-79

Based on USGS Piseco Lake 15' Quadrangle

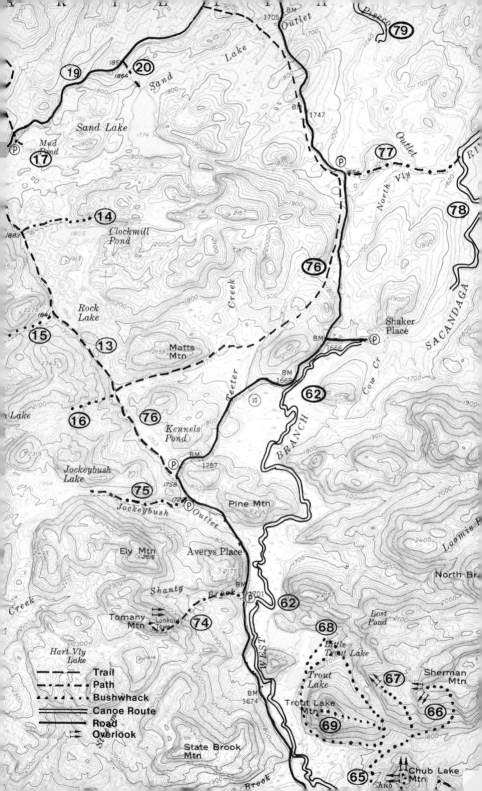

1 Mussey Dam
Short path, walking, picnicking, swimming, fishing

Many of the lovely picnic places line the East Canada Creek. One is called Mussey Dam. Bolt holes in the rock above a natural flume are all that is left of the dam. Upstream on the east side of the creek there is old stone work from the mill.

In this wild and beautifully rocky stretch of the creek, you will enjoy good views both upstream and down. Here the granite faces of the shores funnel the tumultuous stream through a steep, narrow sluice into a deep pool, which is suitable for swimming and fishing.

To reach the spot, drive on the Powley-Piseco Road north of Stratford for 2.5 miles to Hawes Road, a dirt road on the left, west. Drive west on the road for 0.2 mile where it bends sharply right. Here there is room to park off the road. To the left, a path heads south and west toward the East Canada 0.2 mile away. You reach the creek at the flume and mill site. The walk to the creek takes but five minutes.

2 The Abandoned Farm
Path along old road, walking, picnicking, fishing

The dirt road described in section I continues north for a total of 0.5 mile from the Powley-Piseco Road to an old iron bridge over the East Canada. The stream and its banks north of the bridge are posted, but land to the south and west is not. Cross the bridge and walk north up the old farm road that zigzags southwest, then takes a direction of a little north of west as it reaches a plateau. There are meadows both north and south of the roadway which are currently posted. The roadway continues west along the southern edge of the upper field and enters the woods and state land as it continues on to Edick Road and the realm of the southwestern guide in the *Discover* series.

The road leads to a lovely place for the fields abound in raspberries and blueberries. In the field at the crest of the hill, deep mosses and lichens provide a beautiful rug for a picnic. The spot is high enough to attract a fresh breeze and permit distant mountain views.

The soil is so poor that this place is one of those anomalies in which even pioneering species do not thrive; the field has been as it is since someone tried to farm it. The soil is so barren of grasses and shrubs that it is certain the underlying hills are sterile banks of sand, perhaps washed from the great glacial lake that filled the East Canada Valley. Similar sterile banks and fields can be seen in many places from the Powley-Piseco Road.

The unposted water south of the bridge is supposed to have good fishing, and in any event, this part of the creek is delightful. A small island divides the creek downstream of the bridge. You will enjoy both the area of the bridge and the fields to the west as places to sit and watch for birds and butterflies, or you can lie in the deep mosses on the crest and simply watch passing clouds.

3 House Pond

Short path along old road, walking, fishing

Apple trees mark three old farm sites on the west side of the Powley Road about 7 miles north of Stratford. All have been used by campers. A path begins from the middle site, at 6.95 miles, opposite Oregon Mountain and leads in a little over 0.5 mile to House Pond. An easy twenty-minute walk will take you to the small pond, though the path's beginning is well concealed in weeds and brambles at the west side of the small field.

The path immediately becomes obvious as it borders a small marsh, which is overhung with low rock ledges. The trail, level at first, begins to ascend with one steep section. It then climbs more moderately to cross a stream and descend slightly to the pond.

Thank heaven for the beaver who have built a house at House Pond, for they have also restored the dam and reflooded the pond. No longer is it the dry marsh shown on the 1901 series USGS maps or as it was when this guide was first written (1971); and it is even fuller than shown on the 1954 survey. It may again become a dry lake, for the beaver are gone, but there is much to enjoy there now.

House Pond's eastern shore has a dry slope covered with spruce and hemlock and a spot used by campers and fishermen. Most of the western shoreline is swampy, but it is full of wildflowers, pink lady's slippers, and gold thread.

When you first reach the pond, walk south toward the beaver dam; there is a faint path, but just follow the shoreline. What you see is only a third of the pond. After you reach and cross the base of a peninsula that divides the pond, continue along this shore to the far end where you find a stand of hemlock of outstanding size.

4 Brayhouse Gore
Path along old road, walking

An old road heads west from the Powley-Piseco Road 0.2 mile south of the bridge over Brayhouse Brook. The history of the road is fascinating; it wanders through a narrow strip of land called the Brayhouse Gore, which lies on the border of Fulton and Hamilton counties.

In successive surveys, Isaac Vrooman (1768) and Simeon DeWitt (1794) established two different points for the western end of the line that separated the Jerseyfield Patent and the Lawrence Tract. Later surveys produced two more points. It was not until 1883 that Verplanck Colvin determined the correct boundary, adding considerable lands to the state holdings. The Gore was placed in Hamilton County, but not before a road had been built through the disputed lands that private interests claimed.

Today the road begins on private but unposted land, though there is usually a chain across it. You reach Forest Preserve land within 0.2 mile. The old road leads an easy 2 miles northwest to a cabin. Only land around the cabin and another tiny inholding a mile west almost at the county line are private; the rest is Forest Preserve. From the distant cabin, traces can still be found of an old road that led to Punk Hole, described in *Discover the Southwestern Adirondacks*.

Brayhouse Gore is of interest because it is one way into the cluster of little lakes and ponds that occupy a high plateau, bordered on the southeast by Dead Horse and West Creek mountains. The path along the gore skirts the south side of the plateau, but no paths lead from it to the ponds, which lie in a region east of the Powley-Piseco Road and north of Brayhouse Gore. They are surrounded by low hills and are remarkably similar in size and shape. Bushwhacking to them from the gore is a real challenge. The region is bordered on the west by the private lands of Jerseyfield, but Deer Lake, Black Creek Lake, West Creek Lake, Bills Pond, Crystal Vly, and most of Long Lake are in the Forest Preserve. An easier access is described in section 6.

5 The Potholers
Short path, walking, picnicking, camping

Probably the most beautiful of all the picnic places in the southern Adirondacks, the Potholers was named by children who enjoy the individual bathtubs, or potholes, which have been worn in the granite streambed by rocks churned in the waters of the East Canada Creek. The creek is often gentle in summer, but it can be a raging torrent in wet weather.

There is parking along the Powley-Piseco Road both north and south of the bridge over Brayhouse Brook. The charming old iron bridge gave way in the spring floods of 1977 and has been recently replaced by a large, nondescript culvert.

On the north side of the culvert, walk east for 100 feet along the Brayhouse to a lovely, but well-used campsite overlooking its confluence with the East Canada Creek. Continue along the creek on one of the several unmarked paths. The Potholers is a five-minute walk upstream.

The East Canada from the Brayhouse confluence upstream to the stillwater above the Potholers is a series of small waterfalls and many rock slides, making it among the region's most photogenic waterfalls.

In July, the small meadow north of the campsite bursts forth in a spectacular display of more than a hundred purple-fringed orchis. Spikes two to three feet tall bear a myriad of delicate orchid-shaped flowers. Please, do not pick or touch the plants. It is a miracle that these flowers have survived and multiplied with so much traffic. If you are observant, walking these paths will also introduce you to the great variety of mosses and ferns and ground-cover plants that grace the north woods.

The paths all lead to a flat rock projecting into the stream with stillwater above and a series of rapids and falls below. There is one waterfall under which youngsters delight in hiding, water conditions permitting. My children also enjoyed shooting the rapids in inner tubes and tiny plastic boats.

The upper rock is ideal for a cookout and is almost always kept free of bugs by a fresh breeze. Framed by deep moist woods on either side, the rushing stream with its noisy cataracts is an exquisitely beautiful place.

6 Brayhouse Brook
Short path, walking, picnicking, fishing

A delightful, fisherman's path follows the south shore of Brayhouse Brook northwest for a mile or so. It can be just a pleasant stroll or an opportunity to fish. Brayhouse Brook is one route to follow to the high lake country. The path was once a winter road for loggers that led to Long Lake and Crystal Vly. Vly is the local name for a wet place; it is derived from the Dutch word, *vlaie*, and in this region is occasionally corrupted to fly. Since

wetlands or vlies surround the brook farther north, it is best to seek a better access if you want to use the upstream portion of Brayhouse Brook as a guide to the lake country.

Another fisherman's path, this one quite difficult to follow, leads to upstream portions of Brayhouse Brook. Like most of these paths, the beginning is concealed. The start is on the west side of the Powley-Piseco Road in a marshy depression about 75 yards north of a parking spot on the east side of the road 9.65 miles north of Stratford. It is just north of a culvert. The path's entrance would escape all notice if you were not really looking for it; at that, you may have to walk along the road to find it.

Once found, the path is easy to follow for 0.5 mile across the high ground of the shoulder of Sugarbush Mountain to a ledge that is about 20 feet above Brayhouse Brook. The steep bank, covered with hemlocks and shielding the lovely brook below, is a charming discovery. The ledge is rimmed with ferns and mosses. A path drops to stream level, continues on the north bank into the swamps. Walk right across the wet area, heading northwest, and pick up the continuing path which cuts across high ground and descends again to the brook, at the head of the marshes around it. You reach the brook the second time after a 1.5-mile walk that is part path, part bushwhack.

You can follow the brook northwest, using it to guide you to Crystal Vly and Bills Vly, or using one of its tributaries to lead to West Creek Lake, a vly that today is a small pond high on the shoulder of West Creek Mountain. These bushwhack routes are merely suggested on the map, and a third access is as easy as any. Walk the trail to Big Alderbed, section 7, for nearly 1.5 miles, and follow the intermittent stream southwest for a mile. You cross a height-of-land and descend to Brayhouse Brook.

This entire area was once honeycombed by logging roads. For years hunters used them enough to keep paths along them, but they have almost all faded. Bushwhacking this region is a real challenge.

7 Big Alderbed

Trail, hiking, fishing, camping
3 miles, 1½ hours, relatively level

The old logging road to Big Alderbed has been marked as a snowmobile trail, and the route can be a problem for hikers in wet weather. The way

Waterfall at the Potholers

the road was constructed—it was cut into the hillside with no thought to providing drainage—makes it a very wet place to walk.

In dry weather, the road provides a lovely, long walk; and it leads to beautiful places, among them Big Alderbed itself, its outlet (which is the beginning of the West Branch of the East Canada Creek), and an excep-tionally pretty grassy vly through which the outlet flows.

The trail begins from a parking spot on the Powley-Piseco Road, just south of the Powley Place bridge over the West Branch. The bridge is 11 miles north of Stratford.

The trail brings you to a small stream after a half-hour's walk, a second stream a half hour later, and finally, a half hour beyond that, to a beautiful stretch of the Big Alderbed outlet stream. The 2.5-mile walk to this spot is easy, over relatively flat terrain.

When the water is low, crossing the stream is just a matter of hopping rocks, but spring meltwater and autumn rains can make crossing impossible—as the presence of a downed cable indicates.

It is less than 0.5 mile from the crossing to the dam at the outlet of Big Alderbed, a section in which the trail climbs along as lovely a stretch of wild stream as there is in the area. Because the trail is just out of sight of the streambed, you might wish to follow closer to the stream here. Try this as a spring walk, when the beauty of the falls is enhanced by spring floods.

The dam at the end of Big Alderbed is a high one, constructed of a wooden crib filled with large stones. It appears to have been four feet higher at one time. As it is, the level of the lake is higher than the remains of the dam would otherwise make it because of the addition of a beaver dam on top of the manmade structure. There are several large, old beaver houses in the lake. The shores of the lake have been stripped of small trees so that parts of them are quite open, with numerous beaver slides along the steep banks.

Big Alderbed's northern end is very shallow and filled with weeds and stumps, and parts are only mud flats. You will find an amazing number of ducks on the lake in August. High hills rim the lake on both the north and south. There is a good, dry campsite at the east end of the lake, and a fine place for picnicking or fishing.

The rumored path leading to Long Lake has never been found, nor has the one to Blind Man's Vly.

Allow 4 hours or more for the round trip to give time to explore the lake.

8 West Branch of the East Canada Creek
Easy bushwhack

East of the point where the snowmobile trail to Big Alderbed, section 7, crosses the West Branch, there is, barely visible in heavy underbrush, the remnant of another logging road. This one follows the West Branch down-stream and makes a pleasant alternate return route from the Big Alderbed lake.

While it is not easy to follow the old road, it is easy to proceed here if you bushwhack, following the south side of the stream. The walking is difficult, but after half an hour you reach a lovely open meadow framed by the spruce of Big Alderbed Mountain. Another half-hour suffices to walk through the meadow to its eastern end, where there are several short paths, all used by hunters and leading to nearby campsites (some of which are even equipped with well-rusted iron stoves). From the southern end of the meadow, a bushwhack due south for 200 yards brings you back to the snowmobile trail.

The very wildness of the woods and the remoteness of the meadow make it hard to believe that its fall visitors (hunters) are so numerous, but the quiet beauty of this place in summer makes it a lovely area to explore.

9 East Canada Creek
Canoe trip

If the West Branch of the Sacandaga, section 62, is the king of the region's canoe trips, certainly the prince is the northernmost flow of the East Canada. It is extremely accessible, since the Powley-Piseco Road crosses the flow by the Powley Place bridge. North and east of the bridge stretches a large meadow that once was farmland.

It takes only a short canoe trip to explore the still waters of the flow that stretches both upstream and down from the bridge. If you start west of the bridge, you must first cross several small beaver dams in the first half mile. Then the creek becomes choked with alders. If you can push through them, you will find another mile or more of canoeable water. You can continue west on the East Canada for half a mile or north through the meadows that line the Goldmine Stream tributary of the East Canada

Creek. Canoeing this section west of the bridge is dependent on beaver flows and water levels, however.

The stillwater east of the bridge stretches over 1.5 miles and is canoeable even in midsummer when the water is low. Sugarbush Mountain, west of the creek, dominates most of the view from the water on the eastern portion of the trip, and the magnificent stands of enormous spruce are especially lovely. The cool shade they provide and their splendid reflections in the still deep water, occasionally highlighted with the reflected white cluster of elderberry blossoms, make this a painter's delight. Blooming meadowsweet against the blue-green of sweetgale provides a contrast to the gently waving grasses and their graceful cascades over the stream banks. Alders, viburnum, and royal fern fill out the shoreline of this typical quiet upland stream.

You will be amused by the appearance of huge green frogs, sunning along the muddy banks or floating on the weed beds. Their many shades of green more than rival the greens along the banks.

For most of the distance on the east side of the bridge, the creek flows in a north-south direction, paralleling the Powley-Piseco Road but sufficiently far from it that no road sounds intrude. Stop and turn around as you hear rapids downstream. The flow is so slight that even the return trip is a leisurely wilderness experience.

10 Ferris Lake
Dirt road, walking, canoeing

A dirt road over private lands connects the Powley-Piseco Road and Ferris Lake. The mile-long road begins at the northern end of the meadows at the Powley Place, just under 11.4 miles north of Stratford. The road heads east, and walking is permitted along it to Ferris Lake. The owners do *not* want anyone to drive on it. Please respect their wishes. Camping is also not allowed on the private lands near the road. The use of good judgment in this situation will help keep all such places open to the public. While a short stretch of the shore near the road is private, the lake is not.

The lake is almost a mile long, with a charming island and dense spruce-covered shores. It is an especially fine lake to explore in a canoe, and in spite of the small cluster of cabins near the road, it is quiet and isolated.

Waterfall on Goldmine Stream

✓ **11** Waterfalls on Goldmine Stream
Short path, walking, picnicking, fishing

Many of the paths in the southern Adirondacks used by hunters and fisher-men lead to especially beautiful and almost unknown spots. One of the prettiest is the waterfall area on Goldmine Stream. Its beginning is un-believably well concealed.

At 12.3 miles north of Stratford, there is a camping turnout on the east side of the road. Slightly downhill, at 12.45 miles you will see a small grassy meadow, also on the east. Opposite and just south of the meadow look for the path. At present a tree with three blazes marks the beginning. Head west along it, and within 50 feet you will find you are on one of the best groomed routes around, one worthy of the designation "trail." Someone has cleared the deadfalls, using rounds of hemlock to create stepping blocks in wet places.

Five minutes, 200 yards from the road, you reach a good bridge made with two hemlock logs over a small stream. The rounds and trailwork are across the stream. The route is southwest, winding across a low ridge, then contouring west around the hillside—low ground is to your left. You wind generally west, then slightly northwest. There are enormous trees, a few of them dead, though the route has been generally kept clear. Cross an intermittent stream, then start down, briefly, to the outlet of Christian Lake. You cross on logs and stones and jog briefly left and pick up the continuing path which occasionally fades in witch hobble.

Just before the stream, an even fainter path descends south 200 yards to the site of a hunters camp where the outlet of Christian Lake flows into Goldmine Stream. Above the camp, the stream is flat and makes a large bend to the south.

The main path bypasses that bend, heading slightly south of west through spruce flats with the marsh opening up through the trees to the south. You cross a spit of that marsh—upstream it is especially lovely with snags and stumps. The old log crossing is in disrepair, but safe. The path leads along a spruce covered knoll and continues straight at a wet area, heading into dense witch hobble. The route is now slightly uphill and you hear Goldmine Stream. Cross a small ferny field, then bear left from the path within 50 feet and you come out just below the falls.

The falls are a series of charming steps plunging into a walled trough with beautiful ledges for picnicking below. Above the falls, water slides over a smooth golden granite outcrop into a deep pool. The path con-tinues on beside the stream past rapids and little falls for about a quarter mile. It gradually peters out as the streambed becomes gravelly and the valley opens up into a dry meadow with Big Alderbed Mountain rising abruptly to the west.

With the good path, the 1.3-mile walk to the falls takes no more than forty minutes. On the return, stay right at the opening just east of the falls, and head left to avoid the blowdowns and find the path after you cross the outlet of Christian Lake.

12 Christian Lake

Easy bushwhack, fishing, camping, picnicking, snowshoeing

The route to Christian Lake is along a sometimes obvious path, partially obscured by long-downed beech trees. The path follows a draw on the north shoulder of West Notch Mountain. Its beginning is on the west side of the Powley-Piseco Road within sight and 200 yards north of the cliffs on that mountain. Watch for the rocky bed of an intermittent stream. (The spot is 0.4 mile south of a sand pit and is marked with a small culvert.)

You will see no path at first, but climb steeply along the watercourse to pick up the path on its south side. The path climbs steeply for 300 yards and then more gradually as it enters a saddle bordered on both sides by small rock ledges and cliffs. The path continues through the saddle but does not descend to the lake through the obvious draw at its western end. There, before descending, look for several blazes and red markers on trees on your right. The path climbs out of the draw and heads downhill toward the flows at the northern end of Christian Lake. Below the saddle the route is almost due west. Blazes and paint daubs help define the faint path.

After descending to the level of the lake, the path crosses two streams in a wet, wooded meadow, with sphagnum underfoot and hemlock above. Continue west for 50 feet and then swing south to the west shore of the lake, where there are several campsites. The heavily wooded slopes of West Notch Mountain rise above the deep, clear lake on the opposite shore.

This remote, wilderness destination can be reached within forty-five minutes. However, the route is an unmarked path and not always clear, so only attempt it if you feel comfortable using a map and compass. One section of the return can present more problems than any part of the trip in. After leaving the lake, walk north to the wet area, cross it to the hillside on the west, and look for the short steep draw you will climb to return. At present, this draw is identified by unofficial orange markers. *Be sure you pick the proper draw.* A second one, beginning less than 100 feet north of the desired one, leads from the meadow northeast to an impenetrable spruce swamp. It is easy to become confused.

13 Clockmill Corners to Kennels Pond

Trail along an old road, hiking, cross-country skiing, snowmobiling
4.5 miles, 2½ hours, relatively level

The handsomest snowmobile trail in this area for hikers heads southeast from Clockmill Corners, a remote bend in the Powley-Piseco Road almost 15 miles north of Stratford. There is nothing at this valley junction to indicate why or how it received its romantic name.

There are several reasons why hikers find this trail so desirable. For one, it is not freshly cut, but rather follows an old logging road. It also runs down a rift valley, permitting exploration of the valley and its lakes and ponds, as well as allowing access to several other interior ponds and small valleys. The snowmobile trails extend east to the private lands surrounding Kennels Pond, section 76, just off NY 10. Snowmobilers may enjoy the route in winter, but the rest of the year, you will need permission to cross those private lands.

There are two good ways to enjoy the walk through the valley. Either hike the 3.5-mile distance southeast from Clockmill Corners to the abandoned beaver meadow known as Teeter Creek Vly and return the same way to your car, or arrange to make a one-way trek the full length of the valley, a distance of 4.5 miles, with transportation at each end. If you wish to make the one-way trip, ask permission at Avery's Inn or the caretaker either at Kennels Pond or one of the houses south of there. The mile between Teeter Creek Vly and NY 10 is not the prettiest of walking routes because the area has been actively logged.

There is only a 75-foot drop in elevation from the Powley-Piseco Road to Kennels Pond, so the trail, which keeps to high ground through the valley is quite flat and easy. It is possible to make the trip through the valley in not much over two hours, except that there are so many diversions along the way. So no matter whether you choose the round-trip trek or the one-way hike, or plan side excursions, you should give yourself a whole day's outing for this adventure.

The surrounding forests of good-sized and fairly old hardwoods add to the pleasures of the walk. Some of the trees that have succumbed to old age are over three feet in diameter. The trail passes a number of small brooks that flow into the larger streams in the valley as well as several lovely ferny meadows.

Most attractive are the lakes and vlies along the valley or accessible from it. Just southeast of Clockmill Corners, the trail skirts a handsome swampy meadow that appears to have a natural dike across its small outlet. This dike is visible 0.3 mile from the start on the north side of the trail. After 0.5 mile, the little stream turns west to join the outlet of Mud Lake, and the swamplands there are barely visible from the trail.

The trail forks in a weed-filled, open meadow at 1.2 miles. Markings here are poor. The left fork heads toward Clockmill Pond, section 14; the right fork follows the long axis of the meadow to the southeast before entering the woods again on a relatively discernible track marked with only one or two of the large DEC yellow-orange snowmobile trail markers.

At 1.4 miles, the trail skirts just south of a small, unnamed shallow pond, the outlet of which flows southeast through the valley, paralleling the trail, to Rock Lake which is 0.5 mile away. Rock Lake is 0.3 mile long, and because the trail is high on its steep southern bank, you only catch glimpses of its rocky shores through the trees. You will want to leave the trail to see the lake.

A mile south of Rock Lake and within 0.2 mile of Kennels Pond, the trail skirts the southern end of my favorite, picturesque, grassy vly. Called Teeter Creek Vly by natives, it extends 0.3 mile to the northwest.

The snowmobile trail leaves the old logging road in the area of the vly in order to avoid crossing it. Swinging northwest of the vly, it follows the west side on high and dry ground. The northern extension of the trail then circles around the south of Matts Mountain, crosses Teeter Creek and one of its tributaries, and then heads northeast toward the parking turnout on NY 10, section 71. From the turnout north, the snowmobile route generally parallels NY 10 to the Sand Lake Outlet, which it crosses on a bridge before finally intersecting the Powley-Piseco Road. The trail then continues along that road, past Sand Lake, back to Clockmill Corners. While the northern extension holds little interest for hikers, it completes the loop for a superior 13-mile-long snowmobile or cross-country ski trip.

The trail in the vicinity of Teeter Creek Vly keeps snowmobiles from the swamps, but it does not help hikers who have obtained permission to cross the posted land and wish to continue straight to Kennels Pond. Circle the south end of the vly on dry ground and opposite the trail's first approach to the vly, about 200 yards across it, climb the south slope beside the meadow to find the path again. It continues through a hemlock stand to Kennels Pond. The head of this pond is remote and lovely, giving no indication of the roads and buildings hidden on the NY 10 end.

The 7-mile round trip between Clockmill Corners and the head of Kennels Pond can be walked in four hours. Because the Powley-Piseco Road is unplowed, those who wish to ski this route, should, with permission, start their trip from the NY 10 end.

14 Clockmill Pond

Path on old road, walking, canoeing, fishing, picnicking, camping

Clockmill Pond is only 0.5 mile from the fork in the Clockmill Corners snowmobile trail described in section 13. It is so close to both the trail and the Powley-Piseco Road that it makes either a great short walk or a pleasant diversion on the longer trek to Kennels Pond.

As noted in section 13, the snowmobile trail emerges in a small, grassy meadow 1.2 miles from the start. The old road to Clockmill Pond forks from the left side of the meadow, less than 100 feet around its eastern end. In the weeks of midsummer, the point where the old road leaves the meadow may be concealed, but once you find the roadway, the path along it will be quite obvious.

The path is unmarked and leads to the pond's northwest corner. You have to bushwhack along the north side on a promontory that separates the pond from vlies to the north. Nearly all the way along to the north edge of the pond, you will reach its outlet where a man-made rock dam was added to the natural dike. The lake is extremely pretty although the water's warmth indicates that it is not deep. Huge exposed rocks line the southern shore, a lovely spruce-covered island seems to float in the middle of the pond, and many water lilies fill the shallows.

A mill did occupy a site near the outlet but little of it remains. All you will find is a large wheel and gear lying just below the beaver dam that crowns the man-made structure. No historical record has yet been found of the mill or its purpose. All that is known is that it may have existed before the middle of the nineteenth century.

You can easily carry an inflatable boat to the pond; it is a bit of a haul for a canoe, but you can, with carries, get fairly close to the pond, section 20. Exploring the pond by water is great fun; the 0.5-mile stretch of water has several bays and it is easiest to reach campsites on the rocky southern shore by canoe. The inlet stream is canoeable through flowed lands for over 0.5 mile toward Rock Lake.

This path is among my favorite fall walks. Mid-September finds the swamp maples around the pond aflame with dark reds. Camera buffs might delight in the reflection in the tiny pool just below the outlet. A beaver dam at the outlet of the shallow pond just below Clockmill Pond has recently washed away and that small pond is already giving way to new meadows full of lush, tall grasses.

The Powley-Piseco Road

15 Black Cat Lake

Easy bushwhack, hiking, fishing, camping

After following the Clockmill Corners snowmobile trail, section 13, almost halfway along the shore of Rock Lake, a total distance of nearly 2 miles from the Powley-Piseco Road, you will cross a small inlet stream. Seventy-five yards to its east, it is possible, with a vivid imagination, to discern an old logging road on your right. This road follows a small valley between two hills for 0.7 mile west-southwest to Black Cat Lake. The road can be followed to the lake, but whether by advanced path finding or bushwhacking is difficult to decide.

It is essential to have a contour map and compass for this walk. The road climbs a small draw, crosses the height-of-land, and descends another draw to the lake. In the draw on the east side of the ridge, the road bed is to the south of a marshy area and can be followed except in two places. The path fades near the top, then becomes obvious again after passing through a small (thirty-foot-diameter) meadow. Descending the west side, it generally follows a dry streambed into the valley, this time staying to the north of the draw. All signs of the road seem to disappear in the heavy growth of the wet southeastern shores of Black Cat Lake.

I wonder what even prompted the naming of the lake, which is a charming place with a beaver dam and house near the outlet and a dark, evergreen-covered shoreline. Fishermen frequent the lake, and there are signs of campers. Allowing forty-five minutes for the bushwhack from the trail, the pond can be reached in two hours from Clockmill Corners.

16 Iron Lake

Bushwhack, hiking, snowshoeing, fishing

An old road heads almost due west from the logging road that follows the south shore of Kennels Pond at a point 300 yards north of the pond, section 13. The old road starts on private land and ends by Iron Lake, which is on state land. As a bushwhack route, the road bed is even less easy to follow than the one to Black Cat Lake, section 15, so you would be better advised to simply follow the small stream that flows 0.2 mile from a swampy area between Kennels Pond and Iron Lake. From the swampy area it is another 0.2-mile-long bushwhack due west to the lake. It is too bad that there are no real trails here because Iron Lake is lovely, with steep shores and rocky outcrops heavily covered with evergreen forests. However, even walking the shores of the lake is difficult, if not impossible.

The trek to Iron Lake along this route should take no more than an hour from the logging road, or three hours from Clockmill Corners. It can also be reached from NY 10, and with permission, the latter is the recommended approach in winter for snowshoers.

It is also possible to reach this lake from Jockeybush Lake, section 75. Some people have walked the outlet of Black Cat Lake on snowshoes to the outlet of Iron Lake and thence upstream to the lake itself. This approach in summer is impossible because of impenetrable growth of evergreens.

17 Mud Pond
Path, walking

Twenty-three Mud Ponds or Lakes lie within the Blue Line of the Adirondack Park. You might be tempted to fault the lack of imagination on the part of the early map makers, but you will not be able to find any pond so named that is not muddy. This one is a lovely bog to explore and is so close to the Powley-Piseco Road that getting to it can scarcely be called a short walk. The pond lies east of the road and is visible from it. The parking spot at the beginning of the path is 15.5 miles north of Stratford. Look for the pond through the trees on the south side of the road and a little over 0.5 mile beyond Clockmill Corners.

The flora is typical of quaking bogs. Cranberries and even wild calla are to be found. For those who enjoy the special plants that adapt to live in a bog, this is one of the three best bogs and among the most accessible of all those covered in this guide. See Chub Lake, section 65, for details on the variety of bog plants you can expect.

18 Snowmobile Trails to Sheriff and Meco Lakes
Hiking, snowmobiling

Sheriff and Meco lakes are privately owned; permission has been given to route a snowmobile trail to them from the Powley-Piseco Road, connecting with trails on NY 8. It appears that the permission is limited to snowmobilers, so the northern portions of these routes are not open to hikers. The southern portions, on state land, do not lend themselves to cross-country skiing because of distances to travel to reach them over the

East Canada Creek

unplowed Powley-Piseco Road. However, part of one of the two routes is a superb nature walk.

One trail begins on the west side of the road, 100 yards north of the trail to Clockmill Corners. Signs point to Piseco and Morehouse, arrows indicate Spy Lake (the snowmobilers route along the road) and Evergreen Lake. No mileages are given.

The trail heads gently uphill through really good woods. You see a marsh on the left through the trees. The narrow trail heads north through a draw for 0.7 mile, a fifteen-minute walk. Just past the height-of-land, stay left to avoid the blowdowns that seem to direct you right into a very wet area.

You descend to cross a little swale, then walk through a level spruce swamp to emerge a mile and twenty-five minutes from the start at a meadow.

The meadow is partly a sphagnum bog filled with Labrador tea shrubs. Time your trip for early June for their spectacular bloom. Bog rosemary, pitcher plants, sheep laurel, and leather leaf also thrive in the bog.

The trail continues on the east side of the bog, then briefly back in the woods to emerge at a larger flow near the confluence of Meco Lake and Sheriff Lake. Beaver have so flooded the outlet of Meco Lake you cannot cross it in summer. The land to the north across it is privately owned.

The other trail starts just north of the Mud Lake path. This route contours north on a hillside, reaching private land in 1 mile. The trail continues north, arcing west along Meco Lake and through a draw to Sheriff Lake. It is possible to use the western trail past the marsh, then bushwhack (a difficult and not terribly pleasant task) along the marshes that border Meco Lake outlet. You will find several old skid trails. One of them leading just north of east will take you to the eastern trail for a thirty-minute return to the Powley-Piseco Road along it. The trails are only 0.6 mile apart, so the last leg of the loop on the road is easy.

19 Picnic and Camping Spots along the Powley-Piseco Road

As you drive north on the Powley-Piseco Road, you may notice several turnouts that are not mentioned in the list of trailheads or path beginnings. Most of these have been used by campers. Some spots are more handsome than others, and a few are worth considering if you wish to stay relatively close to the road. While they are often used on weekends, they are usually empty on weekdays. Those noted below are especially desirable for their accessibility to the region's walks and canoe trips.

Several campsites can be found in the sand flats beside the road just north of the Powley Place bridge. These were created when the road was reconstructed, when sand was removed from the bed of the dry glacial lake that underlies the lovely meadow north of the bridge.

Three turnouts opposite Sugarbush Mountain to the west of the Powley-Piseco Road between the parking turnout for the Brayhouse Brook path and the Powley Place bridge can all be used for camping. Short paths lead from each to the East Canada Creek.

The northernmost, and probably the prettiest, of the camping spots lies at the end of a short dirt road heading west just under 1 mile north of the path to Mud Pond, section 17. The road leads less than 100 yards to a site beside a tiny stream that cuts through a deep sand bank. To the north the stream flows into a lovely grassy swamp that supports a profusion of turtlehead and purple asters in mid-August.

J 20 Sand Lake
Path, walking, canoeing, fishing, camping, swimming

The Sand Lake path begins on the east side of the Powley-Piseco Road, exactly 2 miles from its northern end. It is an easy walk of about 0.3 mile although the middle section passes through a muddy wet area. The lake is best enjoyed from a canoe, and the carry is short enough to make this possible. There are no paths around the shore.

There is a campsite at the end of the path, which brings you to the outlet end of the lake. The eastern shore is sandy in places and good for swimming. With the shape of a fat C that arcs almost a mile, Sand Lake is one of the larger uninhabited lakes in the region.

A wild bit of exploration extends the canoeing opportunities on the lake. Paddle due south from the outlet for 0.7 mile to the lake's inlet. There is a short carry of 100 yards over the rocky, first part of this stream. Above the carry, though, the stream is open and flat, coursing through flowed lands punctuated by a couple of small beaver dams that require portages. Even in low water this section is navigable, and with little current and much to see, it is easily accomplished. In fact, the small beaver dams only assure that there is enough water for a bit more canoeing.

Another carry over a rocky section marks the end of the flowed lands. Just beyond, a very narrow channel is canoeable for a short way and in high water can be used to enter Mud Pond, so that if the shores of Mud Pond were anything but swamp, you could put the canoe in there, and thus have a shorter carry from the road.

A side stream here, to the south, is canoeable only a short distance. A beaver dam used to keep water in the small unnamed pond drained by the stream. The pond lies between the channel and Clockmill Pond and with a 0.2-mile carry to the west of the stream, you could paddle across the pond. A short carry across the esker at the outlet of Clockmill Pond allows you to take a canoe to that pond. Unfortunately, the drying of this unnamed pond precludes that, but if you canoe the channel, do explore south to see if beaver have once again restored this water route.

Along the Adirondack Park's Southern Boundary

AT THE SOUTHERN edge of the Adirondacks, the Blue Line, which delineates the boundary of the Adirondack Park, is scarcely 20 miles from the Mohawk Valley. Patches of private land are mingled with Forest Preserve lands in the lowlands where fields and timbered tracts are just beginning to return to forest cover. Several areas were reforested with softwoods and conifers, which have now reached maturity. A network of logging roads provides a system of snowmobile trails, but only the few that are notable hiking or ski-touring routes are described.

The trails are in the vicinity of the first road cut from Johnstown west to Salisbury in 1799. A portion of that early route survives as the trail of section 21.

21 County Route 119 to Glasgow Vly

Hiking, cross-country skiing
7.8 miles, 4 hours, 350-foot elevation change

The majority of snowmobile trails in the southern Adirondacks that follow abandoned roads over recently cut land or old farm sites are interesting to hikers only as exercise. The trail that connects County Route 119 to NY 10 is a marvelous exception and surprisingly pleasant. Summer field flowers abound in the open stretches, deep woods shade other sections, and the vlies, or dying ponds, are full of birds and ducks. As a nature trail for spring or fall walking, it is one of the most inviting at the southern edge of the Adirondacks. Even though the route is a favorite with snowmobilers in winter, cautious cross-country skiers can enjoy the long trek.

The western end of the trail begins from County Route 119, 2.7 miles southeast of the intersection of that road and Stewart Landing Road. If you are approaching from NY 10, head west on NY 29, north on County Route 119 to signs for Crystal Lake, a dammed lake on Middle Sprite Creek. The trail sign is just beyond.

Map II: Sections 21, 23-30, 32-34, 36-43, 45, 49-50

Based on USGS Canada Lake, Caroga Lake,
Peck Lake and Lassellsville 7½' Quadrangles

Mud Lake

– – –	Trail
· – · –	Path
· · · · ·	Bushwhack
——	Road
≡≡≡	Canoe Route
⤊⤋	Overlook

N

0   0.5   1.0 mile

Except in winter, it is possible to drive about 1.2 miles along the dirt road from the west. A favorite way to enjoy the trail is to start walking or skiing at this end and have a car waiting at the NY 10 end.

The eastern end of the trail is marked Glasgow Road, which heads west from NY 10, 1.2 miles north of the intersection of NY 10 and 10A. There is a turnaround and parking 0.6 mile from NY 10, and the road is usually plowed to it in winter. Hence the actual trek is 7.2 miles, or 6 miles if you drive part way in from the west. The mileages given on the trailhead signs bear no relation to the actual distances.

Starting at CR 119, you will come to a fork in the road at 1.4 miles; the way right leads downhill 0.15 mile to Tamarack Vly, with a small pond in a large swampy area, pretty enough for a detour.

The marked snowmobile route follows the left fork, heading north for 0.6 mile through a lovely forest of tall cherry trees to a little body of water inappropriately called Mud Lake by local people. It is unnamed on the USGS maps. The lake's lovely southern shore has high cliffs covered with hemlock woods, and you will find several good picnic spots and campsites. The road/trail passes within 50 yards of the lake, and you will see two good paths leading toward it.

Beyond the lake, the trail turns east and descends to cross the lake's outlet. The USGS Canada Lake Quadrangle shows both this outlet into Tamarack Vly, which drains into Middle Sprite Creek, and an outlet directly west to Sprite Creek. Both exist in high water. Just beyond the outlet, at 2.2 miles, you reach an intersection with a trail north, to Stewarts Landing, section 39.

Your route straight ahead curves southeast, traversing land that was once farmed, and the next section is bordered with small trees and many field flowers. In August, you will want to stop and pick blackberries. The trail, still following the old roadway, swings south of east around Tamarack Vly and at 3.0 miles, 0.8 mile from Mud Lake, passes a cabin near a stream. This marks the end of roadways that are still used and the next stretch, in contrast to the first part of the walk, cuts through deep hardwood forest. Then, at 3.8 miles, as you approach Hillabrandt Vly, you will walk through hemlock thickets that appear like a walled corridor carved out of dense evergreen woods.

An old dam, at 4.0 miles, backs up the water of Hillabrandt Vly, and the trail crosses the outlet of the dam. In the 1930s, the vly was a large treeless wet meadow that could be walked through in hunting seasons, when it teemed with partridge. Now the dam holds back water nearly to the limits of the vly, with the exception of brushy meadows on the north and

northeast. Part of the earthen dam has obviously eroded, but beaver have kept the basic structure intact. After a few dry seasons, the vly could return to meadow, for it is only a shallow body of water filled with pond weeds and water lilies, and hardly more than three feet deep. You can easily explore all its recesses on a winter ski trek.

Many ducks nest in the swamps below the outlet dam. The vly has several good campsites, all in the hemlock groves that border it.

The trail proceeds east from the dam, climbs away from the vly, and then turns southeast toward Glasgow Mills, on a relatively level or downhill course. The downhill is nearly 2 miles long and follows what is sometimes a very muddy track. The section is lovely in winter, however, as the woods change from hemlock to mixed hardwoods.

Glasgow Mills is the site of a man-made lake, fairly shallow now as the dam is much eroded. In the late 1800s, there was a large sawmill and a clothespin factory at Glasgow Mills, but evidence of the small settlement is hard to find. The discerning eye can find the dam, but no sign of the huge wheel that powered the mill. Occasional pottery or metal objects protrude from the soil. Walk south along the causeway and look down from it to find a beautiful, tall stone wall that must have been part of the mill.

From Glasgow Mills east the road downhill becomes steeper. At 6.65 miles you cross the outlet of Glasgow Vly; the bridge has nearly collapsed, though it is easy enough to ford the stream. Continue down, still steeply to the parking turnaround at 7.2 miles.

This trail is best as a cross-country ski route. The long gentle slopes are perfect. To make best use of the route with only one car, start at the NY 10 eastern end, climb to Glasgow Mills, vary the route by leaving the trail about half way between Glasgow and Hillabrant vlies and ski down to the dam and causeway at Glasgow Vly. Clumps of evergreens break the frozen marshes. The open pond takes you back to the trail near the causeway at its eastern end.

If you ski to Hillabrant Vly, the return, except for the first 0.2 mile east of that vly, is relatively level followed by a great run downhill back to your car.

√ 22 State Reforestation Area near Rockwood
Cross-country skiing
5-mile network, 2½ hours, 200-foot elevation change

Fulton County trails wind through the state reforestation area near the intersection of NY 10, 10A, and 29 in Rockwood. The mature evergreen forests make a beautiful setting for a cross-country ski trip. Nearly 5 miles of old roads through the area are currently marked and groomed for skiers in a series of loops with several downhill pitches.

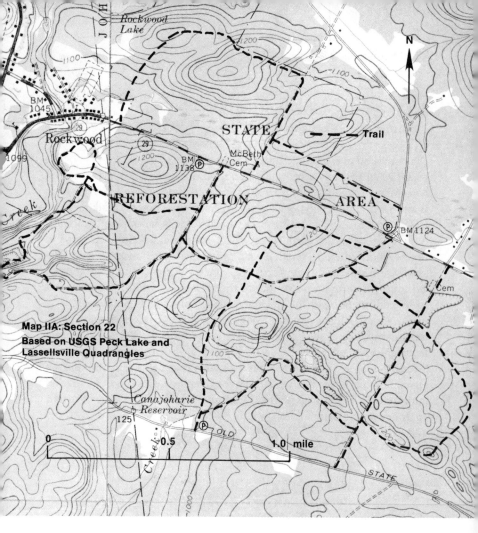

Map IIA: Section 22
Based on USGS Peck Lake and
Lassellsville Quadrangles

There are three parking areas. One at the intersection of NY 10A and 29 serves both the trails north of NY 29 and the loops to the south. Stone pillars, remnants of CCC work in the 1930s, mark the entrances to both, as well as to a third entrance 0.9 mile farther west on NY 29 where there is a second parking area. A third parking area is on Old State Road, which parallels NY 29 about 1.5 miles to the south. To reach the parking area, drive 1.3 miles east of NY 29 at Garoga.

Map IIA details the loops as well as the steep pitches in the trails, which are not too difficult for intermediate skiers. When snow covers the evergreens, no handsomer trails can be found.

Many of the trails are on land belonging to the Canajoharie Waterworks. Trail signs are removed in summer and the area is posted.

23 Glasgow Mills from the South
Path along an old snowmobile trail

An extension of roads north from Lassellsville leads to Glasgow Vly. The route was marked as a snowmobile trail and an alternate beginning was constructed to the trail from a point west on County Route 119. The route is still used, unofficially, but its best use may be as an easy walking route to Glasgow Mills. The trail is exceptionally flat, soft, and well groomed.

Take Green Street north from NY 29, passing at 2.4 miles the road to the St. Johnsville Reservoir. At 3.2 miles turn north on East Road. Depending on the condition of the road, you may drive along it for another 1.7 miles. Here the western spur of the snowmobile trail heads downhill to the right, the road to Glasgow Mills is uphill, straight ahead.

The path along the old road leads gently uphill in a northeasterly direction, then across a long level. The forest contains notable black cherry trees, and the understory of New York and hay-scented ferns is lush. The forest is so open it gives credence to claims that those ferns inhibit the regeneration of cherry stands. After a thirty-minute walk, you will descend fairly steeply to the dam at the outlet of Glasgow Vly. The trail to NY 10 is across the causeway.

Canada Lake Vicinity

CANADA LAKE WAS the first planned community in the Adirondacks. In 1865, the Wheeler Claflin Company bought 20,000 acres in the town of Caroga, two-thirds of the entire township and almost exactly the portion that is now Forest Preserve land. The company needed the forest in order to harvest hemlock bark for tannin, necessary to cure cowhides that were shipped to the area from all over the United States and from South America.

William Claflin owned numerous shoe factories near Boston, Massachusetts. It was easier to ship the cowhides to the forests for curing than to ship hemlock bark or the tanning liquor to the factory sites. Many tanneries sprang up in the wilderness. The tannery at Wheelerville on the inlet of Canada Lake was one of the Adirondacks' largest. It employed as many as 300 men during the two decades after 1865. A small town sprang up around the tannery, which boasted some of the largest leaching and drying sheds in the Adirondacks.

The company also built a huge sawmill at Pine Lake and constructed a plank road to it north from Wheelerville. A plank road was built to connect Wheelerville with Newkirks in the south part of the town. A road had been built from the railroad at Fonda to Newkirks in 1849.

William Claflin saw more profit in forests than those he expected to derive from the tanning industry. In 1866 he constructed a huge frame hotel, one of the Adirondacks' first resort hotels on the northeast shore of Canada Lake. The Canada Lake House was five stories high with wide porches overlooking the water. While Claflin himself spent scarcely any time at Canada Lake—a very wealthy man, he later became governor of Massachusetts—his vision began Canada Lake's long history as a resort area, which has spread to encompass the shores of several nearby lakes.

A small stone dam was built on the outlet of the lake to float logs to mills closer to Dolgeville and factories to the west. The dam created a 4.5-mile-long outlet stream that was navigable. Vacationers were taken along the 7-mile stretch of lake and outlet by a small fleet of steamers, which provided a most elegant wilderness trip.

Two later hotels, the Auskerada, built in 1887 to replace the Canada Lake House, which had burned in 1883, and the Fulton House, which was erected on the south shore in 1888, continued to attract guests to the southern Adirondacks through the first two decades of the twentieth century. Because travel to the lake was by horse and cart, most early visitors came from the surrounding communities. By 1890, visitors from New York

City had discovered the resort, and a colony of artists and writers grew around the shores of the lake. Both hotels have since burned, but the area continues as the hub of one of the prettiest resort areas in the Southern Adirondacks.

Canada Lake is on several lists as one of the "ten prettiest" lakes in the Adirondacks. The lake is on a high plateau, 1500 feet above sea level. Mountains rise steeply from its shores, though these mountains reach less than 1000 feet above the lake, as is typical of southern Adirondack lakes.

Today cottages line much of the lake's shore, but the scenery is the same as that recorded in 1819 by Henry R. Snyder in the first written description of the lake. "The lake, the mountains, and the woods are sublime. . . . The lake is walled in on both sides with mountains, each mountain crowned with a majestic peak raised above all its surroundings, and each peak so placed as if designed to watch over the lake." An anonymous author writing in 1845 thought the lake was "the most romantic spot I have ever visited. The surface of the ground rising back from the shore is covered with large irregularly shaped rocks from five to forty feet in diameter, lying entirely above ground, and often tumbling together in mountain masses, lodges and wedged in like driftwood."

Only the forests are changed. Mr. Snyder recorded that the "north shore of the lake was covered with a primitive forest, the pines, spruces, and hemlocks all towering above the hardwood trees. . . . All through the forest, from the tops of the mountains sloping to the shore of the lake, these majestic kings of the primeval glades stood in their dignity and grandeur." Today, most of the magnificent evergreens are gone.

Tannery and lumbering sites make archeologically interesting destinations. The network of logging roads that were cut to harvest the trees offers some of the loveliest hikes in the Canada Lake area. Many have been reopened as snowmobile trails and currently attract numerous cross-country skiers.

24 Wheelerville Tannery Site
Short path

Parts of the Wheelerville Tannery exist today. A few of the tannery buildings are standing, converted to other uses. The Nick Stoner Inn on NY 10 was once a barn used by the tannery, with oxen kept on the first floor, horses on the second, and hay above. The Caroga Municipal building and the Nick Stoner Golf Club Shop occupy the tannery store, through which a roadway once passed, allowing carts to be unloaded from either side. Some nearby homes once belonged to tannery workers.

The Nick Stoner Golf Course covers part of the tannery site and obliterates all signs of the original buildings there. However, remains of two of the largest tannery buildings in the Adirondacks, a leaching shed 475 feet long and a drying shed 525 feet long can be found beside the inlet of Canada Lake. They were built in 1866. Their foundations are in the woods beside the golf course. Walk along the edge of the woods from NY 10 beside the eighteenth hole for about 200 yards, then head north through the woods toward the stream. You should be able to locate the foundations easily and identify the flume through which wastes from the tanning process were flushed into the stream. Huge piles of iron straps, which held barrels together and bound bunches of hides, can be found west of the foundations.

An alternate way to reach the site is by canoe from Canada Lake, see section 37 for launch directions. Upstream from London Bridge, the bridge over the inlet, new channels have been cut through the flowed lands. The inlet is the middle of the three main streams. It heads south, then east, through the swamps. Pull your canoe out on the south shore at the very beginning of the rapids, where you will find a footpath. The first 200 yards of walking are wet and buggy, but it takes less than five minutes to reach the beginning of the tannery foundations.

An added bonus to canoeing to the site is the opportunity for birding offered by the swamps in the inlet area.

25 Irving Pond from the West

Dirt road, walking, swimming, canoeing, snowshoeing, cross-country skiing

The short road to Irving Pond is currently open to vehicular traffic, but the road is too washed out to permit all but high-wheel-base vehicles. It provides a delightful walk, 0.7 mile long, to a pretty, uninhabited lake, with good canoeing, and several paths along its shores.

Park near the Nick Stoner Golf Course and walk the road north from the parking area. Beyond a group of summer homes, the road parallels the outlet of Irving Pond in a delightful gorge. If you take a right fork within sight of the pond, you can walk or ski along a gated roadway that leads along the south shore of Irving Pond. This trail is mostly out of sight of the pond and connects, at 1.6 miles, with the trail to Bellows and Holmes

lakes, section 26. A path across the dam on the east side leads to adventures in section 28.

Walking around the pond to favorite promontories or picnic spots is fine, but the best way to enjoy the pond is with a canoe. From the water you can see Hogback Mountain looming above the pond on the northeast. All of the shores have heavily wooded slopes, the water is very clear, and the sand bottom makes for good swimming.

The pond is a natural one that has been enlarged so that it is nearly 1 mile long. James Irving erected a dam at the outlet in 1855 and operated a sawmill nearby. Next to the mill he built a substantial home, where he and his family lived for nearly two decades.

The present high dam was used to regulate water flow into Canada Lake when that lake was used for power. In recent years, the floodgates have been closed so the water level has been relatively constant. Now, as soon as you leave the bay by the outlet, the shoreline seems wild and untouched, and only a few twisted stumps in the shallows indicate earlier logging or changes in water level.

In dry times, when there is little flow over the spillway, you can cross the dam to pick up a path on the west shore. In high water, it is safest to hop across on the rocks well below the dam. The same route is easier to follow in winter on snowshoes or skis when you can cross the frozen surface of the pond.

In winter, the road to Irving Pond provides an excellent beginning for a trek around the pond. In spring, when the woods are still too wet for walking, the road is a great place to hunt for wildflowers. Beside the outlet road you will find a splendid array of spring flowers, among them lady's slippers, may apples, and trilliums.

26 Irving Pond and Bellows Lake to Peters Corners

Snowmobile trail, hiking, cross-country skiing
6.6 miles, 4 hours, 550-foot vertical rise

East of Caroga Lake a marked and maintained snowmobile trail follows old roads north from Benson Road to Irving Pond, then northeast to Bellows Lake. Past Bellows Lake and near Holmes Lake, the trail intersects an old logging road that also runs north from Benson Road, this one from

Irving Pond Outlet

Peters Corners. The trail connecting the roads describes a semicircle suitable for either hiking or cross-country skiing. The area is beautifully varied, with fields, open woods, and dense forests. There is a great range of wildflowers, making this an especially pretty trip in spring and fall.

To walk the through route, you need a car at each end. This may also allow enough time for side excursions. The eastern end of the trek is at Peters Corners, 6.5 miles east of NY 10 on the Benson Road. You can drive north for 0.2 mile and park along the roadside.

The western end of the trail begins along a dirt road that leads north from Benson Road 2.8 miles east of its intersection with NY 10 in Caroga. (The roadside trail signs give incorrect mileages.) In summer it is possible to drive along this road for 0.4 mile. At the end of the dirt road, the trail heads north through the woods, first crossing a wooden bridge over a small stream, then turning west of north along level ground. After a slight rise along a small hill, in an area that can be quite wet, the trail, still following the bed of an old logging road, intersects a similar road at 1.1 miles near the southeast corner of Irving Pond.

(An alternate way to reach the southeast corner is described in section 25. It reaches the southwest corner after 1.6 miles.)

At the intersection, head north along the old logging road. After crossing a bridge over a small inlet stream of Irving Pond, the trail turns east toward Bellows Lake. The entire stretch is gently uphill through a deep evergreen forest. The distance between the intersection and the closest approach to Bellows Lake is 1.4 miles. The trail does not actually lead to the lake; at this point, at 2.5 miles into your through trek, you will have to bushwhack a short distance to see the water. Except for part of the north shore, Bellows Lake is surrounded by marshes. There is a large flow of water from Bellows to Irving, draining also the swamps northeast of Bellows. In winter, it is delightful to ski out onto the lake (stay away from the outlet end, which may not be completely frozen because of the large volume of water) and ski toward the northeast to the marshes that surround Frie Flow, the principal inlet of Bellows Lake.

The trail continues northeast, coming close to the lake again at 2.7 miles. Beyond Bellows, it crosses an intermittent stream, heads northeast, uphill, then curves east, climbing more steeply to reach a height-of-land at 3.85 miles. Watch as the trail descends, for 0.15 mile from the height-of-land, just before the trail begins to descend fairly steeply, there is a path back left, leading northwest toward Little Holmes Lake. See section 27.

The trail now descends fairly steeply to intersect an old logging road at 4.6 miles. Turn right, south, toward Peters Corners, passing at 4.7 miles the remains of a sawmill, see section 27 for a description. Beyond the intersection, the trail turns south along the Holmes Lake Road; the route is clear and obvious, but not well marked. You cross three intermittent streams in the vicinity of the saw mill ruins, and reach boulders barring vehicular traffic from the south at 5 miles. At 6 miles the trail to Pinnacle Road, section 81, forks left, east, at 6.4 miles there is a possible parking area, and Peters Corners on the Benson Road is at 6.6 miles.

√ ## 27 Holmes Lake and Little Holmes Lake
Trails and paths, hiking, camping, fishing, cross-country skiing
2.6 miles to Holmes Lake, 1¼ hours, 350-foot vertical rise

Holmes and Little Holmes can be considered excursions from the through trail of section 26, or destinations from the east end of that route at Peters Corners. There really is no good public parking at this end; and the road is often muddy and difficult to drive. Four-wheel-drive vehicles do drive northwest for 1.5 miles, but do *not* try it in an ordinary vehicle. There is an open area 0.2 mile from the Benson Road where you can pull off in summer.

At 0.65 mile, a snowmobile trail forks right, east, to Pinnacle Road. This end of that trail is too brushy for pleasant walking. The road begins to climb, bordering the handsome Holmes Lake Outlet, which becomes a deep hemlock gorge with little waterfalls. At 1.6 miles, you reach the end of private land and boulders bar the way for further vehicular traffic.

The roadway is occasionally muddy and wet, though great walking in dry weather. It passes a drying beaver meadow, a stark and bristly place of alder stumps. Then the outlet becomes a hemlock-filled gorge again—delightful—and at 1.7 miles reaches the first of three intermittent streams that flow from Hogback Mountain on the west. At 1.8 miles you are in the middle of several rows of foundation piers, the remains of an old mill. You can find a turbine amid intriguing foundations that lie right beside the trail.

The mill was built by Russell E. Holmes, for whom the lakes were named. It had four turning blades to manufacture chair rungs from hardwoods for shipment to a furniture factory in Gardner, Massachusetts. He owned about 1000 acres surrounding Holmes and Little Holmes lakes, and first built a sawmill on the shore of Holmes Lake in 1888. A settlement filled the clearing just short of the lake, boarding facilities for twenty-four people.

Holmes Lake

He built the turning mill after the turn of the century and ran it until his death in 1915. His widow sold the acreage to a Michigan company that logged off all the hardwoods and returned it to the state for back taxes, a common practice.

Beyond the turning mill site, the trail angles uphill and right and at 2 miles reaches the fork to Little Holmes Lake. If you continue straight, the route can still be wet and muddy. You cross the settlement clearing at 2.4 miles and reach Holmes Lake at 2.5 miles.

Holmes Lake has pretty good trout fishing, several good campsites beneath hemlock trees, and a fairly open shoreline so that walking around the lake is inviting (just stay back from the marshes at the western end). Holmes Lake is a gem, nestled beneath a steep hill. The lake reflects a deep green hue in summer. Birding is good here as well.

If you turn left at the intersection north of the mill site, heading up the narrower trail, you climb fairly steeply for nearly 0.6 mile, heading due west. Just as the grade becomes easier, before the height-of-land, a path whose beginning is somewhat concealed forks right. This narrow path along an abandoned roadway is fairly easy to follow as it leads northwest through a draw, then downhill for 0.6 mile to within 100 feet of the west shore of Little Holmes Lake, where it disappears among fallen trees and underbrush. Little Holmes Lake is even more of a gem than Holmes; at one-third the size, it is held at the base of steep slopes. The bookkeeper for the Holmes factories thought the setting resembled the crater of an extinct volcano.

You can continue north among the evergreen trees along the lake's west shore to where the path reappears along its outlet. The path crosses the outlet a few hundred feet downstream from a beaver dam and curves east contouring around a hillside to the east, staying above a vly to the northwest called Frie Flow. The path leads to the site of a turn-of-the-century logging operation beside a stream entering the vly from the east. Remnants of the logging camp, stone fireplaces, and foundations and a huge rusted boiler that gave steam power to the mill can still be found on the edge of the flow.

The logging road used to continue north to Duck Lake, where it met other roads from Stoner Lake and Pine Lake.

√ ## 28 Stewart and Indian Lakes

Marked ski trail, hiking, camping, swimming, picnicking, snowshoeing, cross-country skiing
2 miles, 1¼ hours, 450-foot vertical rise

The marked ski trail to Stewart and Indian lakes, northeast of Canada Lake follows an old logging road. This traditional route to the two lakes makes delightful walking. The beginning of the trail is off Green Lake Road, a north turn from NY 10 immediately west of the bridge over the channel between Green and Canada lakes. Drive north for 0.6 mile to the fork where the shore road curves around the north shore of Green Lake. The dirt road straight ahead leads to the trailhead. There is parking 200 yards along the road.

Walk from the parking area north for 200 yards to the marked beginning of the trail on the right. The trail descends to cross the outlet of the Fish Hatchery Pond, heads generally east, climbing gradually for over 0.5 mile. You cross a small stream, then climb steeply in a draw. (This section always seems too steep and narrow on the return when you are skiing.) The trail heads a little north of east as it levels out. Continue on the level for 100 yards or so, looking for open water through the trees to the north. The trail does not touch the lake, so you have to leave the trail and bushwhack 200 yards or so to it.

The trail skirts the swampy area on the southeast corner of the lake, then swings north around the lake. Just beyond the swampy area, at 1.4 miles, you can bushwhack west along the north shore to a lovely rock promontory and camping spot. This is the best spot from which to see the tiny lake, which is nestled below the humps of the Camelhump.

The snowmobile trail continues another 0.6 mile to Indian Lake, curving northeast, and finally north to approach that shallow body of water. The time stated to reach Indian Lake does not allow for a stop at Stewart.

If you are adventurous, you might want to try to find the cliffs north of Indian Lake from which there is a view of Stewart Lake, Kane Mountain, the Camelhump, and a small part of Canada Lake. Bushwhack around the west shore of the lake—it is marshy and rough going—and cross the outlet. From the outlet of Indian Lake, head due north for less than 0.5 mile through woods that are relatively open after a short span of dense growth near the shore. Climb 280 feet to the escarpment; you will still have to search about for the cliffs.

A favorite snowshoe loop approaches Stewart Lake as described, then crosses the lake to its far western lobe. Then continue west through the draw between the humps and descend, traversing the hillside beneath the cliffs that range across the southern hump. Your course is generally southwest to intersect the ski trail.

√ 29 Irving Pond to Stewart Lake via Prairie Lake
Bushwhack

A flagged path follows an old road over this route, but the path has received so little use that it is very difficult to follow, so treat this 2-mile trek as a bushwhack. After you have made the trek once, however, finding the path will be obvious.

Start at Irving Pond, section 25, and cross the dam, or cross the stream below the dam, depending on the water level. On the west side of the dam there is a path that curves around the shoreline, back 50 yards from it. Watch carefully, for it turns northwest, following the draw, along what is obviously an old road here. Signs of the roadway diminish, but you continue uphill through the draw and at the height-of-land turn north to contour north, almost without changing elevation until you are about a mile from the dam.

At this point you will have to go northeast to keep the mountain on your right. Head northeast, but downhill slightly, then east. High hobblebush obscures your approach to Prairie Lake, which you can best approach by leaving the path and heading toward the high and dry ground of the lake's northwest shore. The path and the old roadway it follows has

all but disappeared. It heads due north up the east side of the draw that drains into Prairie Lake's western end. From here it is but a 0.5-mile bushwhack, uphill, north, then northwest over a small rise to intersect the Stewart and Indian lakes trail, section 28, southeast of Stewart Lake. It is not too difficult to locate the old roadway near Prairie Lake, but finding the place where the path meets the upper trail is so difficult, unless you have been there before, that it is best to make this trek in the direction described.

✓ 30 Otter Lake

Path, walking, fishing, picnicking, canoeing, cross-country skiing, snowshoeing

The walk to Otter Lake is hardly more than a stroll but the 0.5-mile-long lake is beautiful and fun to explore. Trout fishing has been good in the lake, and you might want to carry a canoe or inflatable boat.

A large private inholding touches a narrow stretch of the south end of the lake, but the rest of the shoreline is state land. Two routes lead to the lake. A private road extends past Fish Hatchery Pond, see section 28, towards the camp. No vehicles are permitted on the road, but walkers have not been stopped. Follow the road to its end at the Otter Lake Outlet where there is a footbridge just upstream from a logging ford. A path leads along the east shore of the outlet and cuts away from the route to the camp, about 100 yards from the camp. It leads to state land along the east shore of the lake.

It may be better to follow the west shore of the stream, avoiding the camp and circle south of the cove at the lake's outlet. From here you cross a lovely hemlock covered promontory and reach the lake's western shore. You will find an intermittent path of sorts that circles the lake.

31 Eastman Lake

Bushwhack

There is no path to Eastman Lake today, although in the early part of this century there was a logging road to it through the inlet valley of Otter Lake. Old maps name this body of water Oxbarn Lake, some say there was an oxbarn constructed there for the logging operation. One old-timer disputes this derivation, claiming that the name Oxbarn on the 1890 USGS

View to the west from Kane Mountain

map predates the logging activity. He says that two surveyors were rechecking their figures in a local bar, desperate for names for the myriad lakes in the region, and pulled this one out of the air. The origin of the more recent name, Eastman, is equally mysterious.

Eastman Lake, a pretty little pond ringed with low hills, is due north of Indian Lake. You can reach it by using the Stewart and Indian lakes ski trail to reach Indian Lake, and then bushwhacking. A course of true north from Indian Lake, keeping to the west of the swampy area, is best, but you should note that this requires keeping a straight course in rugged terrain for a distance of over a mile, not a small feat. The walk to Indian Lake takes over an hour, the walk around to its northern shore over a half-hour, and the bushwhack to Eastman another hour at least.

The inlet valley of Otter Lake is a less difficult bushwhack route, and takes about two and a half hours. Walk to Otter Lake and along either shore to the northern corner of the lake. Since the east shore trail leads first through marshes, the west side is more direct in spite of the fact there is no real path along it. From the north corner, it is easy to pick up a path that heads northeast along the inlet, which is the outlet of Stewart Lake.

Follow the stream northeast for 0.5 mile, where it bends sharply uphill to the right, out of the northeast-southwest trending valley, to the southeast toward Stewart Lake. Follow its north bank for 0.2 mile. Traces of

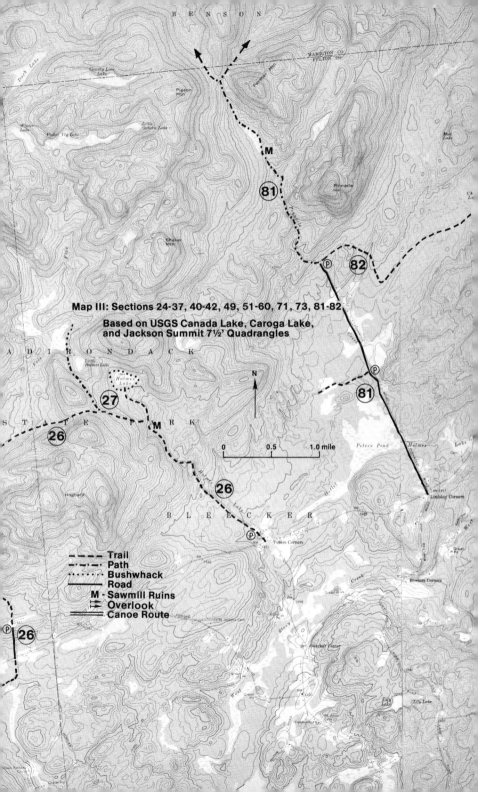

Map III: Sections 24-37, 40-42, 49, 51-60, 71, 73, 81-82

Based on USGS Canada Lake, Caroga Lake, and Jackson Summit 7½' Quadrangles

- - - - Trail
······· Path
········ Bushwhack
———— Road
M - Sawmill Ruins
Overlook
Canoe Route

0   0.5   1.0 mile

paths from Otter Lake extend this far and make travel easier if you can find them. Strike due north between two knobs on the ridge between the Stewart Lake outlet and the outlet of Indian Lake, which flow quite close together here. Cross the Indian Lake outlet and bear northeast for about a mile. You are climbing the long ridge of the hill. The terrain levels out and Eastman Lake becomes visible through the trees a couple hundred yards below you to the right. There are occasional views from the ridge as you climb.

When you do finally reach the lake, you might wish to imagine how it looked before the turn of the century, before the forest was logged. Old timers remember that there was no vegetation below the trees on the east side of the lake, and there was a large blue heron rookery on the shore. After the trees were logged, heron were never seen at Eastman Lake again.

32 Green Lake to Pine Lake

Trail, cross-country skiing
1.2 miles, 40 minutes, relatively level

A ski route has been marked from the Fish Hatchery north of Green Lake to Pine Lake. It generally follows an old roadway along the base of Kane Mountain, describing an arc heading north then angling west. It stays up on the slopes above the deep valley and passes through a lovely mixed forest. At 0.8 mile it intersects a trail to Kane Mountain, which branches back left, or south. The ski trail descends through a hemlock stand, curves around Pine Lake Campground, and heads west to 29A.

In winter a sign on NY 29A denotes the western trailhead. From it a route is marked that heads east, through the open field, along a road in the trailer park, behind trailers, across a bridge over Pine Lake outlet, then to the trail. Because the route is through the trailer park, there is no summer use at this end.

33 Kane Mountain

Trails, hiking, distant views
0.5, 0.8, and 1.0 mile respectively, 580-foot vertical rise

Kane Mountain has three trails to the summit fire tower, which is manned from May through October. On really clear days the view unfolds to include the mountains of the Silver Lake Wilderness interior, with Hamilton Mountain visible in the northeast. The view north along the mountains that rim the Sacandaga River Valley ends with the hills behind Piseco Lake and T Lake Mountain. The most spectacular vista is across the Mohawk Valley, southeast to the Helderbergs and south to the Catskills, where Black Head, Black Dome, and Thomas Cole stand out as a cluster of giant rounded peaks. There is no view from the wooded summit.

One trail starts from a painted boulder on Schoolhouse Road. There is room for three cars to park at the trailhead. The steep route, 0.5 mile long, follows the telephone lines up the mountain along a trail so rutted and eroded you could not miss it. The 580-foot climb can be made in half an hour.

A slightly longer, 0.8-mile, less steep trail begins at the parking area between Green Lake and the Fish Hatchery Pond. It winds generally west up the hill turning south across the summit to the tower. It is the easiest of the three routes and takes but half an hour for the climb.

A third route, the longest of all, about 1 mile, begins from the campground at Pine Lake, north of Kane Mountain. Because the campground is off limits in summer, start on the marked ski trail from Green Lake, section 32. Follow it for 0.8 mile to the intersection with the tower trail. The latter swings south to climb rather steeply toward the ridge. The last segment generally follows the long axis ridge of the mountain to the tower. The route is through beautifully wooded country and deer are often seen here in summer.

34 Morey Road to Stewart Landing

Hiking, cross-country skiing
5.5 miles, 3 hours, relatively level

Immediately after 1810, settlers could purchase 1000-acre homesteads in the Glen, Bleecker, and Lansing Patent for 18 cents an acre. Homesteaders moved from the east along Benson Road to Five Points, the area around the intersection on NY 10 just north of the present community of Caroga Lake. A road from Five Points, now called the Morey Road, extended west into the wilderness south of Canada Lake Outlet. That road is now marked as a snowmobile trail and it extends for 5.5 miles to Stewart Landing.

The western 1.2 miles of the trail are described in section 38. Because of the enormous distance to drive around and make this a one-way trip, the trail is best enjoyed as a round trip from either end. Drive east on Morey Road beyond the last house. The road is plowed this far in winter. Head gently uphill, generally east, crossing the head of a draw in 0.8 mile, and a second draw at 1 mile. The route now ascends gradually as it continues east. In summer the woods floor is covered with ferns and Solomon's seal and sessile merrybells.

At 2 miles, the trail dips slightly, curving north to cross a small stream, then returns to an easterly direction to follow the north side of the stream. Shortly, open meadows appear to the left of the trail. This is a farm site that was abandoned before 1850. It takes about an hour and a half to walk the 2.8 miles to the meadow, where in summer, old pumps and pipes, iron wheels, and other remains of the farm can be found.

The trail continues from the northwest corner of the meadow, and makes a short but steep descent (difficult on skis) to the level of a huge spruce swamp at 3 miles. The trail then arcs north around the swamps and crosses a small knoll as it heads southwest, reaching a large bridge over a portion of the swamps at 4.3 miles. If you are coming from the east, turn around here. If it is winter, head out into the very extensive open vlies to ski along them.

35 Pine Lake

Path along an old road, walking, canoeing

Once you get past the buildings at the south end of Pine Lake, just off NY 10 north of Canada Lake, you discover a most attractive mountain lake. Pine Lake can be explored peacefully by canoe or from the path that edges its western shore.

To reach both the canoe launch site and the start of the footpath, turn east of NY 10, drive to the lake and turn left onto the road that follows the lake's western shore for 0.5 mile. Park at the end of the road.

Launch your canoe and paddle north; it is possible to continue in this direction for a mile, until you reach a swamp dotted with the stumps of trees killed when the level of the lake was artificially raised by the dam at the southern (outlet) end. Linear patterns of the roots of upturned stumps are beautifully silhouetted against the quiet water of the lake's upper end, which seems to disappear into the swamp. You will be surprised and delighted by this area's apparent remoteness, and if you enjoy photographing nature, you can certainly spend several hours exploring the stump gardens and water plants.

The footpath also runs for 1 mile from the parking area toward the lake's northern end. Following a well-constructed old logging road that was in places raised above swampy areas on a base of large stones makes a pleasant hour's walk. The wildflowers of the deep woods, ferns, and saprophytes enhance the short woods walk, and there are lovely views east across the lake.

The path also gives access to the two low hills just to the west that are lined with huge boulders and short cliffs. No walk along the lakeshore would be complete without exploring some of these, and in fall, the view from the tops of some of the knolls is especially nice. Surrounded by lovely hills, Pine Lake is dominated by Kane Mountain on the south, Pine Mountain on the east, and a small hill local people call "Roundtop" to the northeast; all cast magnificent reflections on the quiet waters of the lake's northern end.

Two streams drain into the lake, both passing through swampy valleys. Paths lead to both from the path along the shore, but consider these bushwhack explorations.

36 Negro Lake
Snowshoe bushwhack

The best way to enjoy Negro Lake and the two other swampy lakes in the area south of Canada Lake is on snowshoes when you can walk across their surfaces. However, Negro Lake is a true quaking bog, so it deserves a summer visit. For that, canoe up the long inlet channel of Canada Lake into which the outlet of Negro Lake drains. Head east, climbing about 100 feet to the level of Negro Lake, which is no more than 0.3 mile from the channel.

A winter trek can be much more extensive; and if you spot a car at the parking turnout at the end of the road along the south shore of Canada Lake, you can make a through trip, passing two other small ponds in addition to Negro Lake. The distances are short, but the landscape has a reputation for being confusing, so the way always seems longer than the map shows it must be.

Start on Morey Road, section 34, and follow that trail east for a mile, to the second draw you cross. It points in a west-northwest direction, and you climb only about 40 feet in elevation from the trail to reach the level of Mud Lake. Mud Lake is only a quarter mile from the trail, and it is no more than 200 yards long.

In winter, cross Mud Lake to its outlet and follow it northwest for 0.2 mile, then head toward magnetic north, zigzagging around high ground to reach Negro Lake. Alternatively, you can follow the frozen outlet of Mud Lake northwest for 0.4 mile (the USGS incorrectly shows the outlet) to a small pond that was only a small marsh on the USGS. Still following the outlet, you reach another vly and head north to reach the outlet of Negro Lake at about 0.8 mile from Mud Lake. Use that frozen stream as a guide to head east to Negro Lake.

From Negro Lake, head north to climb the shoulder of an unnamed hill. Follow the ridgeline of the hill, angling slightly east to a cliff where there is a fine view of Negro Lake. There is also a view east-northeast along the steep northern face of Sheeley Mountain.

Continue on high ground, winding generally northeast, over the hill to bluffs with views of Canada and West lakes. Descend the long ridge northeast directly to the parking area at the end of the south shore road. The 3.5-mile trek usually takes nearly four hours, mostly because it is so easy to get confused on the way.

Canada Lake Outlet and Sprite Creek

THE NINETEENTH-CENTURY dam at Stewart Landing on Sprite Creek was designed to serve the lumber mill on the outlet of Canada Lake, but the long, navigable channel it created provided a great adventure for vacationers staying at hotels on the eastern end of the lake. Imagine a day-long excursion on a thirty-foot steamer with ladies wearing hoop skirts and wide-brimmed hats to protect them from the sun and smoke belching from the steamer's smokestacks. Often the steamers would pull a chain of rowboats full of extra passengers.

Today's adventures along the outlet and Sprite Creek are not as elegant, but there are several trips that certainly can be as much fun.

The outlet of Canada Lake, Sprite Creek, flows west to join the East Canada Creek, which courses south to the Mohawk River. The drainage patterns in the vicinity of the lake are curious because you have no sense of a height-of-land in the area. Just south of Canada Lake, the Caroga Lakes flow south toward the Mohawk, entering that river a dozen miles east of the confluence of the East Canada Creek. But, just north of the Stoner Lakes, which are the northernmost source of Canada Lake, water flows into the West Branch of the Sacandaga. That river makes a circuitous route north, then east, to empty into the Hudson at Luzerne, over 50 miles as the crow flies from where Canada Lake waters enter the Mohawk.

37 Canada Lake Outlet
Canoe trip

Four hours of paddling are required for the round trip from Canada Lake, through Lily Lake, to the dam at Stewart Landing and back. It is a handsome canoe route, especially in spring or fall when few motorboats are in the water. The presence of motorboats and the growing number of cottages on the north shore of the outlet stream keep this from being called a wilderness, but sections still appear remote and lovely. The state has recently acquired the south side of the outlet from the dam east to the Caroga town line, so that shore will keep its pristine character.

There are two public boat-launching sites on Canada Lake, one at a fishing access on West Lake Road, and the other, for which there is a small fee, in the vicinity of the store at Canada Lake, on the northwest side of NY 10, less than 0.2 mile from the bridge over the channel between Canada and Green lakes. To reach the fishing access, take the left, or south, turn from NY 10, 1 mile northwest of that bridge. Take the right fork 100 yards from NY 10 and park on the west side of Sawdust Creek, the outlet of Pine Lake that provides a short channel to West Lake.

From West Lake, canoe south to Canada Lake then west to Lily Lake, which is surrounded by state land. There is a campsite on the south side of Lily Lake, below the hill. Most of the Lily Lake shore is heavily wooded, low, and wet, so there are only a few places on state land where you will find a spot near the water that is high and dry enough for camping. Lily Lake has the namesake lilies and a good variety of other water plants. Wood ducks and mergansers are often found in the pickerelweed, and loons frequent the area regularly.

West of Lily Lake, the channel narrows, threading between rocks and twisted stumps. The stream is smooth and easy, with little current in summer, and the few rocks in the channel are not apt to bother canoes. Look for the rocks at the western end of Lily Lake and in the large narrow horseshoe bend 2 miles beyond Lily Lake. The channel is so narrow in several places that it is difficult to imagine how loaded steamers made it the entire way to Stewart Landing dam.

Beyond the horseshoe channel, the outlet flows through a broad flooded area, zigzagging through the marshy growth. The last straight stretch leads to the dam; to the right of the dam there is a sandy beach to pull out your canoe.

The water in Canada Lake is regulated by the dam under the regulation of the DEC. Water is lowered somewhat in October. In November the level of the lake is allowed to fall four feet, and at this time the channel is barely navigable by canoe. The water level is restored as soon as the ice is out—usually some time in late April. There is a gauge on the bridge between Canada and Green lakes that measures water level in feet above sea level. Summer level is supposed to be just under 1543 feet, but it has been consistently higher in recent years. Below 1541 feet, a canoe trip down the outlet becomes difficult; below 1539 feet it is impossible.

From the launching site behind the store at the eastern end of Canada Lake to its outlet into Lily Lake, the distance is 2.5 miles. From there to Stewart Landing dam is almost 4.5 miles. The distance from the fishing access through West Lake to the entrance to Lily Lake is almost 1.5 miles.

Canada Lake Outlet

To start the trip at Stewart Landing, take County Route 119, which connects Lasselsville and Emmondsburg. Stewart Landing Road is 0.5 mile east of Mallet Hill Road, which is the most direct route from NY 29A near Stratford.

38 Along Sprite Creek
Short path, picnic spot

The nineteenth-century mill dam across the outlet of Canada Lake at Stewart Landing was superseded in 1912 by a higher dam built a quarter mile downstream. This one channeled water through a long wooden flume to a generating station downstream on Sprite Creek. The ten-foot-diameter flume with its huge metal rings has disappeared, but the remains of the surge tower, which controlled the rush of water from the lake, still stands west of Stewart Landing near Sprite Creek.

A roadway leads past the surge tower, now only a huge cement scaffold looming incongruously in the woods. You can use the roadway as a route to the tower or to the nearby creek. It is a good route for a short walk and provides access to a handsome section of stream with a series of little waterfalls and rapids.

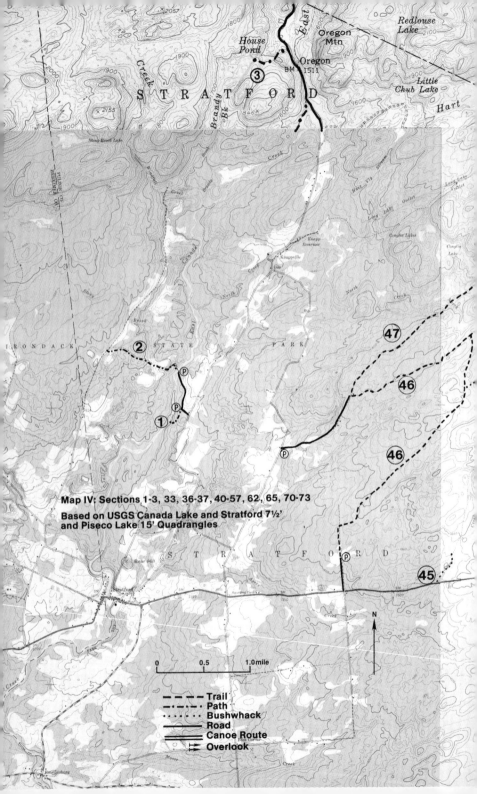

Map IV: Sections 1-3, 33, 36-37, 40-57, 62, 65, 70-73

Based on USGS Canada Lake and Stratford 7½'
and Piseco Lake 15' Quadrangles

– – – –	Trail
–·–·–·	Path
·········	Bushwhack
————	Road
══════	Canoe Route
►►►	Overlook

0   0.5   1.0mile

N

Power House Road is 0.5 mile east of Stewart Landing Road, see above. Start measuring when you turn on Power House Road. You pass Youker Road at 0.8 mile, then at 1.1 miles, near the height-of-land, turn south. Some of the land adjacent to this road is posted. At 1.3 miles turn left to the surge tower. If you continue straight, or southeast, you will notice that the land on the west is posted. This road leads to Middle Sprite at the ruins of an old stone bridge. A lovely waterfall is just downstream. Land to the east along the creek is not posted. Walk upstream to enjoy rapids on the creek.

39 Stewart Landing to Mud Lake

Snowmobile trail, cross-country skiing, hiking
1.4 miles, ½ hour, relatively level

This trail makes use of a 1.3-mile connector route that brings the possibility of several variations. The trail begins at Stewart Landing, just west of the dam, and heads south, crossing Sprite Creek on a high bridge. It climbs slightly, heading southeast through high ground. This is second growth forest, and several old logging roads branch from the trail, which is well enough marked so there should be no confusion. At 0.6 mile, a trail forks left.

The left fork leads along a well defined old roadway that heads a little north of east, on high ground. The way is level for the first 0.5 mile, then there is a descent of about sixty feet in elevation to a bridge over an un-named stream. This is the same bridge that is the destination of the trail west from Morey Road, section 34. Hence the first possibility, a through walk from Stewart Landing to Morey Road.

If you continue straight ahead, south, at 0.6 mile, you descend gradually for 0.7 mile to a second intersection, this one with the trail from County Route 119 near Crystal Lake to Glasgow Vly, section 21. A right turn, west, brings you across the outlet of Mud Lake and uphill for 200 yards to the first of two paths north toward the lake. The second is easiest. If you continue southwest beyond Mud Lake, you reach County Route 119, at 3.4 miles. Obviously, you could start this journey from County Route 119, using this route in reverse to reach Stewart Landing.

The third variation on this link would be a trip from Stewart Landing to Glasgow Vly and NY 10, a distance of 7.2 miles. For this you take the left, east fork, at the second intersection and continue as in section 21.

Between Stratford and Pine Lake

A DOZEN LONG, gently undulating routes have trailheads on NY 29A between Stratford on the west and Pine Lake on the east. Here snowmobile trails have been laid out along a network of old logging roads. In the past decade these routes have been discovered by cross-country skiers, and, on a few, skiers outnumber those on machines. With care to keep out of the way of machines—a not-too-difficult task since even on weekends a skier will encounter no more than a half dozen machines—these trails offer a well-groomed wilderness trek. Some of the forests near the highway are small and scrubby from repeated logging, but within a short distance, maturing stands are encountered. The routes are wide and easily skied; there is enough change in elevation to keep them challenging. The terrain is varied with a number of ponds and beaver meadows.

A few of these routes are muddy and wet in summer, making them less than desirable as hiking trails. However, a September walk on most of these trails is blazing with color, a not-to-be-forgotten experience.

Several connector trails wind east-west between the major routes. Those that are marked by the DEC are described in the text. There are several other unofficial trails, several of which intersect roads on a private inholding surrounding Ayers Lake. These connectors are noted in the text, but not described.

√ 40 Nine Corner Lake

Hiking, cross-country skiing, snowshoeing, fishing, camping, swimming
1 mile, ½ hour, 280-foot vertical rise

This snowmobile trail along an old road leads to one of the prettiest lakes in the region. However, the fact that it has been limed and kept stocked with trout has also made it the most popular fishing lake around. In summer you will find at least half a dozen cars parked at the trailhead on weekends. Unfortunately, camping pressure has led to degradation of part of the shoreline.

However, the offerings here are incredibly diverse, from earliest spring when the trail sides are good places to find wildflowers, to summer when the swimming is good, through fall when the woods glow with color, and into winter when the route beckons cross-country skiers.

In winter, snow obliterates signs of shoreline destruction. Skiers can enjoy the frozen surface as an easy way to explore the lake's many corners and the spruce covered islands in the northern bay. They will also enjoy most of the downhill run on the return from the lake, though the last quarter mile approaching the trailhead is steep enough to give this route at least an intermediate rating.

This is one lake where a boat is very desirable, and the width and grade of the trail make it possible to carry a canoe or inflatable boat to the lake. From the water, the lake has many hidden and unusual spots, deep bays that are hard to reach by land, and small islands. You may sometimes see loons diving and reappearing in the northern reaches. The water is cool and, like most lakes stressed by acid rain, exceptionally clear.

The trailhead is on the north side of NY 29A, just 250 yards west of its intersection with NY 10 at Pine Lake. There is parking on both sides of the road. The trail rises 180 feet in the first 0.3 mile, then crosses the outlet stream in an area of lovely little falls. At 0.9 mile there is a cut-off path to the outlet.

The outlet end of the lake has smooth rocks from which people like to swim and a campsite that is high and dry. Very few of the lake's many corners are visible from here, but paths have been pushed along both the north and south shores. The snowmobile trail continues west, skirting the lake, section 41, to intersect with the trail of section 43. From it you can head north to reach several picnic spots on rock outcrops high above the water.

41 Nine Corner Lake to Burnt Vly

Snowmobile trail, cross-country skiing
2.3 miles, 1½ hours, 300-foot elevation change

It is 1 mile to Nine Corner Lake from NY 29A and 1.1 miles from that road to the western terminus of this trail, near Burnt Vly, section 43. Hence the shortest ski trip using this segment would be 4.4 miles. From the first approach to Nine Corner Lake, 0 mile, the trail continues west, around a knob, then swings back close to the lakeshore. It leaves the lakeshore at 0.7 mile, heading southwest through a steep draw. This nearly 200-foot descent in under 0.5 mile is a challenge for beginning skiers. However,

Nine Corner Lake Outlet

it is a fairly wide trail and the run is not as difficult asthe return on the Nine Corner Trail.

The trail heads generally west, climbing then descending from the shoulder of a hill to the north—but nowhere as steep as the stretch southwest of the lake. Skiing west to east to reach the lake is not difficult. Either way, this route brings you close to the western lobes of the lake; and you will enjoy skiing the lake's surface and exploring its islands and peninsulas.

42 West Lake

Hiking, cross-country skiing
1.4 miles, ¾ hour, relatively level

A new route has been cut expressly for snowmobiles to connect the road to West Lake with the trail to Nine Corner Lake. For a short walk in spring and summer, the trail is surprisingly interesting. In winter it makes a fun ski route—and if you add it to the trek to Nine Corner Lake you have a full day's outing.

The northern end of the trail is opposite the trail to Nine Corner Lake, on the south side of NY 29A, 300 yards west of the intersection with NY 10 at Pine Lake. The southern end of the trail is on the road from NY 10 to West Lake, about halfway between the lake and the boat-launching site described in section 37. There is parking at that site in both summer and winter.

The trail heads south from NY 29A, crosses the outlet of Nine Corner Lake, skirts the outlet of Pine Lake (which is also the inlet to West Lake known locally as Sawdust Creek) and the flows beside it, then continues in deep, rich woods for 1.4 miles to the West Lake Road. The route is west of south, then almost due south, though the trail curves about a lot to keep a level contour.

The route is a fine nature trail (pileated woodpeckers are often seen near its northern end), and the terrain is so gentle walkers of all ages can enjoy it.

Skiers should note that there are three fancy snowmobile bridges on this stretch, which they should approach carefully, for the short slopes beside them can seem unexpectedly steep.

43 Third, Fourth, and Long Lakes

Hiking, cross-country skiing, camping, fishing, picnicking
8.7-mile loop, 5 hours, 200-foot vertical rise

Skiing along two old roads leading to Third and Fourth Lakes has remained consistently good, and hiking them seems even better than it did a few years ago. Beaver meadows no longer so severely flood the trail, especially in the area of Burnt Vly. Snowmobile trails have been designated along each of the roads that head north within a short distance of each other on NY 29A. They intersect north of Third Lake, not far from Spectacle

Lake, and there is a connector between the two trails north of Pleasant Lake. A loop using both trails makes a super winter trek.

There is a parking turnout for the eastern trail on the south side of NY 29A, opposite the trailhead. It is 3 miles west of Pine Lake and 0.7 mile east of Pleasant Lake. Signs at the trailhead give the destination as Spectacle Lake (6 miles) and Dexter Lake (6.5 miles) with no hint that the trail first passes Fourth and Third lakes.

The western end of the trail branches from the East Shore Road at Pleasant Lake, about 0.3 mile north of NY 29A.

The eastern half of the loop is the more interesting because it passes close by Burnt Vly. In fact, if conditions are right—that means the vly is safely frozen—use this route alone as a route to Third and Fourth lakes and vary the return by skiing the southern section of the vly just north of NY 29A.

The trail starts north through the woods, jogs to the east to avoid the marshes of Burnt Vly, then back west to the vly at 0.8 mile, where you have your first view of the vly. It is here that you can head due south for 0.5 mile over the frozen vly to vary your return on a one-way trip.

The trail climbs nearly 100 feet in elevation in the next 0.3 mile until at 1.1 miles, the trail to Nine Corner Lake forks right. You jog west and at 1.3 miles reach a second of the open marshes with handsome stumps that give Burnt Vly its name. The trail stays east of this vly, then at 1.9 miles the trail comes quite close to the stream at the south end of a third vly. The trail again swings east around this vly, returning to cross Burnt Vly stream at 2.5 miles.

A gentle rise takes you at 2.8 miles to a cross-over trail to the western leg of this trek. The cross-over is 0.6 mile long and intersects the western trail 1.3 miles north of its start near Pleasant Lake. Another rise, then the trail becomes level at 3.5 miles. Here, look for Goose Egg Lake to the west of the trail. It is a tiny drop with thickly wooded shores and lies about 200 yards from the trail.

Beyond, the trail swings to a northeasterly direction and at 4 miles intersects the trail from Arietta, section 56. You have to follow this trail east for 0.2 mile and leave it to approach the shores of Fourth Lake. The route north, however, does approach quite close to the western end of Third Lake at 4.2 miles. At the northwest corner of the lake, the trail turns northwest, downhill, to intersect at 4.5 miles with the western trail from Pleasant Lake.

In summer except for your first approach to Burnt Vly, the trail is no longer as flooded by beaver work as it was a few years ago, but there is no guarantee beaver work will not flood the trail again in the next few years. If you use this route in summer to reach the site of the settlement between Third and Fourth lakes or the shores of Fourth Lake, note that beaver have flooded a section of meadow between the lakes. Buildings from this settlement were still standing in 1953, and the logging camp here was occupied as recently as 1945 when this area was last logged.

The western route leaves the road beside Pleasant Lake and heads northeast on an old logging road, generally north beneath a small hillside to the right, then between two small hills. There are signs of past logging, not enough to disturb the winter scenery, but enough to make the route dull and uninteresting in summer.

At 1 mile, the trail reaches an intersection where an unofficial connector route used by snowmobiles forks west, left, to intersect the trail on the west side of Pleasant Lake. The trail continues north, intersects the crossover trail to the east leg, then bends northwest to skirt a spruce swamp. The trail now makes a long loop to the west, returning northeast and descending to reach Long Lake just short of 3 miles. Long Lake is a beautiful little body of water with flat shores that sport several dry rocky spots for picnics.

The trail swings northeast past Long Lake, again through sometimes-muddy sections. Just before the trail crosses the inlet stream at 3.9 miles, you will see a path to the right, or east, that constitutes a shortcut to the eastern snowmobile trail. If you miss this junction, no matter, for there is a second intersection 0.2 mile farther on. Here the left fork heads north to Spectacle Lake, section 44, and the right fork is the east trail that heads south to Third Lake.

Fourth, Third, and Long lakes are all long and narrow with their major axes running southwest to northeast. The area surrounding them is flat, and their shorelines are low. Fishing is dominated by warm-water species. The summer round trip to Long Lake is a total of 6 miles, requiring little more than two hours because of gently rolling terrain. Allow one hour to walk from Long Lake east to Third and Fourth lakes. Since these trails are also accessible by trails from the east and NY 10, section 56, via Spectacle Lake, and from the west via Waters Millpond and Dexter Lake, there are several opportunities here for long one way treks. All of the routes are very easy to follow on skis, especially after snowmobiles have packed the route.

Waters Millpond

44 Spectacle Lake from the South

Hiking, cross-country skiing, fishing, snowshoeing, camping
1.7 miles beyond Third Lake, 1 hour, relatively level

The snowmobile trail past Fourth and Third lakes, section 43, extends north through very flat, wet ground to Spectacle Lake. The distance from NY 29A to Spectacle Lake is stated as 6 miles; and while it is not that far to the lake, it is certainly that far to an area where the ground is not too swampy to camp. Other trails to Spectacle are preferable for hiking, but this route is useful to combine with them, especially in winter.

From the intersection of the two trails north of Third Lake, section 43, continue northwest for 0.3 mile to a fork that you may not even spot. The way right is an old road, not presently marked as a trail. It led to the eastern side of Spectacle Lake and the trail of section 71, but you could not follow it now. If you want to make that connection in winter, it would be best to continue on the left fork until it reaches the shores of Spectacle, then ski to the eastern end of the lake—a long detour.

The way left heads northwest, then north, contouring on high ground above Spectacle Lake and the marshes that lie south of it. Beyond the trail's closest approach to the lake, 1.3 miles from the intersection, the trail heads west, paralleling the shoreline for 0.3 mile. The old road, which the trail has been following, used to swing south around marshes at the outlet of Spectacle Lake to a logging camp 0.3 mile from the lake. The present trail crosses the marshes and continues northwest through a shallow draw to the outlet of Dexter Lake, section 47. At this point, 0.7 mile from Spectacle Lake, the sign points back to the Burnt Vly Trailhead, giving the distance as 6 miles, and underestimating it by 0.8 mile.

Hikers will undoubtedly use shorter routes to both Spectacle and Dexter lakes; and skiers will find this is equally long. Even the snowmobiles seem to use it infrequently.

45 Ayers Lake Outlet

Bushwhack

Ayers Lake is in the center of a large private inholding, but a part of its outlet near NY 29A is in the Forest Preserve. The outlet crosses NY 29A, 5.5 miles west of the junction with NY 10. Follow the left, west, side of the outlet upstream through surprisingly lovely woods. You reach a large flooded beaver marsh in about fifteen minutes and can easily continue along through the open forest on its shore.

46 Waters Millpond

Hiking, cross-country skiing
3.2-mile ski trip one way, 2 hours, 300-foot vertical rise

Two snowmobile trails lead toward Waters Millpond and intersect 0.6 mile to its west. One begins at Seeley Road, which heads north from NY 29A, exactly 1 mile east of Stratford. The other, which also heads north from NY 29A, is an extension of Avery Road, which is 1.3 miles east of Seeley Road. The latter has little interest for hikers. For some reason, snowmobilers even seem to avoid it, so it is not very attractive for cross-country skiers.

In winter, Avery Road is plowed for 0.35 mile, as far as the last house. Park here and ski the continuing road for 200 yards to a dead-end sign. A chained road, the traditional route to Waters Millpond, forks northeast. Stay straight on Avery Road and watch for a snowmobile trail sign on your right 0.25 mile beyond the last house. (The continuing woods road leads north to state lands, gradually petering out as it goes.) The trail is a narrow route, cut to bypass private land but it goes through a swampy area for 100 yards, wet walking for sure. The new and old routes rejoin in another 500 yards, then the trail continues northeast, following the roadway over gently rolling and undistinguished terrain. At about 2.3 miles there is an unmarked right fork to Ayers Lake, one of the unofficial connectors that uses logging roads near that lake. At 2.9 miles you intersect the trail from Seeley Road to Waters Millpond.

The Seeley Road approach to Waters Millpond is the more interesting by far. Seeley Road is plowed in winter and the southern half is paved. At the northern end of the paved section, 1.8 miles from NY 29A, a dirt road branches to the east, extending through private lands for 1 mile before ending. It is possible to drive this section in summer; in winter, the best time to use this route, the trail begins at Seeley Road at an intersection known as Potter Homestead. Ski along the almost level, wide dirt road for 1 mile from Seeley Road in an arc to the northeast to a trail junction. Signs indicate the way left is the trail to Dexter Lake, section 47, and the way right leads to Waters Millpond. The way right continues a little north of east past a private camp, curves north on a wide track that is mowed in summer, and then enters state land at 1.6 miles. A brief uphill follows—the rest of the route is very flat.

The trail is through second-growth forest, which is returning to maturity. The woods are especially nice in winter with the contrast of dark patches of evergreens. The trail takes a narrow winding route, and at 2.4 miles reaches a handsome patch of woods and traverses a shelf on a hillside of hemlock. At 2.6 miles, a marked right turn indicates the trail to

Avery Road. A sign back the way you have traveled indicates Potter Homestead, erroneously giving the mileage as 3.0 miles.

The way ahead leads in 0.6 mile to Waters Millpond. Continue straight, still northeast, shortly passing an open vly surrounding North Creek on the right. This vly has been recently flooded by beaver; the trail on the south side of the vly is under water so you will have to bushwhack briefly through the woods. The snowmobile bridge over North Creek is also flooded, cross it and work left on new paths. Beyond the vly, the trail climbs beside a small gorge surrounding the outlet of Waters Millpond. You reach an open field at 3.2 miles.

Swamps surround the pond, which, though a natural one, was enlarged some time prior to the 1901 USGS survey by a flood dam built for logging operations at its outlet. That dam no longer holds water back, hence the pond's entire northwestern section, which must have been only a shallow flooded area then, is now just a large swamp. The wetness makes it difficult to explore the perimeter in summer, but there is open rock for picnicking and swimming where rock shelves lead down to water north of the dam. Beaver have been at work, restoring the dam, and open water currently covers a much larger area than a decade or so ago. You might see heron that nest in the marshes at the north end of the pond.

In summer, with the trip shortened by 1 mile, the 2.2-mile walk to Waters Millpond takes under an hour. The trail continues to McKinney Vly and intersects the Dexter Lake Trail, section 47. If you are using this route to approach the pond from the west, note that you have to look about for the trail west of the outlet at the south end of the field where it enters the woods—summer grasses conceal it.

The trail to McKinney Vly heads west out of the field and circles the pond, well back from it. At 3.4 miles, the trail angles sharply left; the path straight ahead leads again to the shore of Waters Millpond. The trail, following an old road, enters a draw, curves around it and descends to the level of McKinney Vly. Turn left again. The trail follows the south side of the vly, just in the trees back from the edge of the vly. It intersects the Dexter Lake Trail, section 47, at 3.9 miles. Note that if you use this route to walk in the opposite direction from Dexter Lake, the place where the trail leaves the vly is hard to distinguish. Look for a cleft in the hillside just past the head of the vly. Head uphill, past a fortress rock, then around the headwall of the draw to a height-of-land that is almost within sight of the marshes surrounding Waters Millpond. It takes about twenty minutes to walk this connector.

One more connector makes it possible to vary a winter trek, but the route is through swamps and marshes, precluding summer travel. No sign marks it, but if you cross Waters Millpond to the east you will see open marshes along an inlet stream. The trail, sometimes following an old road, disappears, and you continue across the open marshes. There is a second pond with open water; you cross to its south side just to the west of it. Continue over open marshes until the stream narrows and you enter the woods again. Follow the south side of the narrow outlet of Long Lake, rising 40 feet in elevation. Here, the trail disappears, and you will probably find it easiest just to ski east through the trees for the last 0.2 mile to Long Lake. You reach the southwest corner of the lake at 4.2 miles, just over a mile from your first approach to Waters Millpond. You will find the trail from Pleasant Lake on the south side of Long Lake.

With two cars, you have a 7 mile loop connecting Seeley Road and the east shore of Pleasant Lake, or an even longer loop through the Burnt Vly trail, see section 43. With one car, you have a 7.9 mile loop past Waters Millpond, northeast to the Dexter Trail, section 47, and return.

√ **47** Dexter Lake

Hiking, cross-country skiing
4.8 miles, 2½ hours, 400-foot vertical rise

The left fork, 1 mile from Seeley Road, section 45, leads in 3.8 miles more (not the 6 miles indicated on the sign) to Dexter Lake. The route is relatively level and the walk so easy that it takes about two hours to reach the lake's outlet. The walk or ski to Dexter Lake can be combined with a trek to Waters Millpond or Knapps Long Lake, sections 46 and 48, and Dry or Spectacle lakes, section 72.

The trail generally heads northeast, following an old but wide road bed through second growth forests. The beginning is flat and dull and often wet. At 0.5 mile from the fork (1.5 miles from Seeley Road), the trail reaches state land. The route continues through land that has been logged within the last couple decades; the trail stays left, well marked, at three intersections with old skid roads. At 1.2 miles, the valley of North Creek is low on your left. The trail crosses a broad drainage area, then heads steeply downhill to the big bridge over North Creek at 1.5 miles.

The trail skirts a large marsh on the outlet of Dexter Lake, which here joins North Creek. You walk under huge hemlock, looking out at the marsh with its huge beaver house. You struggle to cross a marsh that is not even indicated on the USGS on a falling beaver dam at 1.75 miles. Pick up the trail directly north of the dam and continue with high ground to the left and ledges on the right through a small draw down to McKinney Vly at 2 miles. (The connector trail to Waters Millpond is just before you walk out into the open vly.)

McKinney Vly once had a flood dam for logging. Beaver have dammed it several times since and the trail is routed across logs that span a break on one dam. It is easier to go 100 feet west to the outlet and cross the stream that forms the vly. Stay on the west side of the vly and push through the high grass for 100 yards or so until you see the continuing roadway/trail heading northwest. (There are markers once you are back in the woods.)

The trail now heads northwest, climbing gently beside the outlet of Dexter Lake. Within just a few minutes you see a new vly on your right with stump reflections and a new beaver house. Ledges line the hill on your left, west, as the trail turns northwesterly to climb the hillside above the outlet stream. Tall, straight maples and black cherry make a handsome canopy over the trail—the mature forest contrasts with the first part of this trek. At 2.6 miles, the route levels out, then begins a long, gentle descent. Short of 3 miles you begin to see the marsh surrounding the outlet to the east. This marsh stretches north along the outlet for nearly a mile. Adventuresome skiers will enjoy varying the trip to Dexter with a loop along its frozen surface.

This part of the route is much pleasanter walking, with ledges on the hillside, a clearer trail, open woods, and hints of the marsh. At 3.5 miles, the trail takes a northerly course, pulls away from the marsh, and finally curves northeast to reach Dexter Lake at 3.8 miles.

At Dexter Lake you will find loons in summer. Because of beaver work, the lake has several outlets. Cross all of them to find a trail marker indicating the trail you have just followed, again with erroneous mileage. The route northwest along the shores of Dexter Lake leads to Dry Lake and NY 10 in 4.1 miles, section 72. A third route, southeast, leads across a small gorge, then east, uphill, traversing the draw between two low hills to reach, at 0.5 mile, the outlet of Spectacle Lake.

A few rocks in the clearing below and to the west of the outlet mark the foundations of a small settlement, and some stones placed across the outlet indicate a man-made dam. Apple trees in the natural meadow at the outlet suggest that the site was inhabited for a period of time.

Remote and pretty, Dexter is a favorite lake with many and a desirable camping destination. The northern shores are gently sloping and dry. The lake is the hub of several routes, and although all are long (this one is the shortest), they are easy to walk and ski.

48 Knapps Long Lake
Path along an old road

Knapps Long Lake lies about 0.6 mile west of Dexter Lake, section 47. An old road from the Powley-Piseco Road on the west passed Knapps Reservoir and led to Dexter Lake. At present the western beginning of the old road is posted. Since all begin on private land, they are not described in this guide. However, Knapps Long Lake is fascinating and might be a desirable destination for those who choose to camp at Dexter Lake.

Starting where the snowmobile trail to Dexter Lake described in section 47 crosses Dexter's outlet, walk along the western shore on an informal path for 150 yards. A path leaves the shore at right angles, following an old logging road west to Knapps Long Lake. You climb a hill heading a little north of west and then continue through a draw between two low hills. Stay close to the southern edge of the draw, below lovely cliffs that range to thirty feet in height.

The path descends from the draw on a gentle, long slope to a swampy area near the northern end of Knapps Long Lake. Mark the place well for your return for the beginning of the road is overgrown and difficult to find coming from the lake. Allow thirty minutes for the one-way walk between the two lakes.

The lake stretches northeast for 0.5 mile; it is long and thin and full of stumps and little islands, which make it appear like either a rotting swamp or a romantic wilderness depending on the lighting. There was a settlement at the outlet of the lake, little of which remains. Scrub forest surrounds the northern shores, so walking there is difficult. The best campsite is by the outlet where the settlement stood.

49 Burnt Vly Stream
Snowshoeing or cross-country skiing

A barred roadway leads south of NY 29A, 2.8 miles west of Pine Lake. It led to an inholding that has recently been acquired by the state. The roadway is broad and easy to ski and leads south, descending slightly, for 0.5 mile to the edge of Burnt Vly. In winter, you can ski a wonderland of frozen marshes. Head either upstream, where the marshes stretch out for nearly 0.5 mile or downstream for nearly a mile toward West Lake. Here the open meadows are broken by patches of alders, which sometimes can be difficult to push through. Clumps of balsam and spruce border the marshes upstream giving variety to the ski trip.

50 From Pleasant Lake South toward Stewart Landing

Cross-country skiing
3.7 miles, 1½ hours, relatively level

Two marked snowmobile trails head south from NY 29A in the vicinity of Pleasant Lake. They join and continue on to Stewart Landing. You can ski both, making a 7.3 mile jaunt if you have a car at either trailhead; and since the trailheads are only 1.1 miles apart, you can walk between them, making the trip over both routes with one car. After the snowmobiles have packed the trail, this makes a great outing, requiring three and a half hours. The terrain is varied, much of it relatively level, with some runs, and only one really steep pitch on either leg.

The eastern trailhead is 3.3 miles west of Pine Lake or 0.6 mile east of the outlet of Pleasant Lake; the western trail is 0.5 mile west of the outlet. Starting on the western leg, you head south through mixed forest and along gentle slopes, then descend to a huge bridge at 0.6 mile over the outlet of Pleasant Lake. South of the highway, that outlet flows through two enormous marshes, and the two legs of this route circle around them.

The trail continues east of south at 1.1 miles, another roadway forks right. You go left, heading east, and at 1.7 miles reach an intersection with an erroneous sign. The right fork leads to Stewart Landing, but it is only 2 miles away. You turn south, still descending, and at 2.2 miles reach the edge of a huge spruce and balsam swamp. It is level and pretty skiing through the 0.3 mile of swamp. Then you climb again and wind generally south. At 3.5 miles you reach a circle in the trail within sight of the road. The marked trail is a left, east, fork and leads to a plantation and a steep descent to the road, opposite the Stewart Landing Trail, section 39.

If you choose the eastern and slightly shorter leg for the return, you turn right at the intersection and go east on high ground for 0.7 mile, gradually curving to the north. As the trail takes on a more northerly direction, it traverses a series of ups and downs, including one steep descent to a crossing of the Burnt Vly stream that is but 0.2 mile from the highway.

Along the Stoner Trail

NORTH OF CANADA Lake, NY 10 is often called the Stoner Trail after the trapper who spent most of his long life, from 1762 to 1853, in Caroga Township. Nick Stoner, a major in the War of 1812, did not lay out the course of the road, but he did act as guide to the first party to survey the route. Stoner's biographer, Jeptha R. Simms, enlivened the trapper's reputation with such fantasy that his name has always been associated with the route.

In the early 1800s, New York State was anxious to survey the Ox-Bow Patent, land adjacent to Piseco. The only roads toward that part of the wilderness headed north from Johnstown. Lawrence Vrooman and James McLallin were commissioned in 1810 to survey an extension through Caroga to Piseco, and Nick Stoner was the guide for the survey party. That road was never built, and it was not until 1841, after a second survey, that a road was constructed along the route drawn by the 1810 part.

Simms's *Trappers of New York*, written in 1850, tells of many of Stoner's adventures on the lakes and streams near the road. Simms described this section of the wilderness as having "a primeval look. Its majestic forest lords and advantageous water powers must in time invite a thrifty artisan and hardfisted yeoman to subdue and cultivate it. It abounds in waters the most limpid, and breezes the most invigorating. The lakes and their tributaries are stores with an abundance of delicious trout; and if not walled castles, stately mansions may yet rear their imposing fronts in these glens; to be known in the future ages as the rivals of the far-famed glens of Scotland." How surprised Simms might be to discover that parts of the wilderness are as wild and untamed as when he first saw them.

The Stoner Lakes, called the Stink Lake by Stoner and his companions are the most northern of the lakes that drain into Canada Lake. There is some ambiguity about the names of the three lakes; some refer to them as East, West, and Upper, though the two western lakes are sometimes referred to as Middle and East.

The section of NY 10 that roughly parallels Stoner Lake outlet, from Pine Lake to the Stoner Lakes, holds half a dozen adventures.

51 Broomstick Lake

Hiking, picnicking, camping, cross-country skiing, snowshoeing
0.7 mile, ½ hour, 300-foot vertical rise

The traditional route to Broomstick Lake, along an old roadway, was marked as a snowmobile trail, though it is no longer so designated. It is so short, however, that it makes a good winter trek for novice snowshoers or cross-country skiers. Hikers the rest of the year will find much to see along the route.

The trail begins on the west side of NY 10, 1.1 miles north of Pine Lake. You proceed a little south of west for about half the distance to the lake, then head more to the north, where the trail curves along the shallow ravine through which Broomstick Lake outlet flows. Here, beside the trail, you can find many native wildflowers that are distinctive of the deep woods, including pink Lady's slippers in spring and rattlesnake orchid in mid-summer.

The trail crosses the head of the peculiar ravine and then passes through a small ferny meadow, a stretch of woods, and finally a swampy area just below the beaver dam at the foot of the lake. The swamp is full of bottled gentian in August. If you cross the dam to the eastern shore, you will find a charming camping spot under hemlocks and one of the southernmost stands of Labrador tea in the Adirondacks.

Broomstick Lake was erroneously named Goose Egg on some of the early maps, but it is not evident that either name fits its shape. One of the more interesting historical notes connected with the lake is that one of the earliest movies ever made, the silent film *Last of the Mohicans*, was filmed on its shores. At least one resident of Canada Lake still remembered playing the role of an Indian in the film. A stockade was erected on the promontory across the ravine that is now the lake's best campsite.

The story of the ravine beside the trail is curious. Rumors persist that it was created by a gigantic explosion that was part of another movie script done by the same producers, Blazed Trail Productions. It certainly does not appear to be a natural feature, but its real history may never be known.

◡ 52 Snowshoe Trek to Nine Corner and Broomstick Lakes

Bushwhack

Expert winter travelers, those who need no trail, may enjoy reaching these lakes by way of a 3-mile-long bushwhack loop off the marked route. The bushwhack and return by trail takes about four hours to snowshoe, which leaves enough time for a picnic.

For the bushwhack, follow the Broomstick Lake trail about 0.3 mile, until it swings north. At that point, leave the trail and head west-southwest through a developing draw. You are heading for the valley between two small hills to the north and south of your route. You climb rather steeply and notice that a small ridge separates your draw from one to the north by about 100 feet. Follow whichever seems easier; for they join as you approach the height-of-land. Sharp ledges line the hill to the north. You climb about 340 feet in 0.8 mile. Continue in the same direction downhill; you reach a handsome hemlock grove on a small rise in the lowlands east of the lake's northern lobe. You can cross the rise or go around it either way, for all paths lead to some point on Nine Corner Lake's irregular shoreline. The hill with ledges to the north continues west to border the lake, and the natural draw to its south makes an easily defined route for the cross-country trek.

When you reach Nine Corner Lake, walk out to the islands in the northern lobe, which provide a hemlock-and spruce-covered shelter for a picnic. From the islands head north up the ridge of the hill; the route is relatively steep, climbing 280 feet in 0.2 mile, but will take you past ledges with winter outlooks and views of Lily Lake and the Canada Lake outlet. From the outlook just below the crest, head 40° east of magnetic north to Broomstick Lake, using the northeast slopes of the hill to guide you. It is 0.8 mile between the lakes. Broomstick lies just 20 feet lower than Nine Corner. Cross Broomstick Lake to the beaver dam at the outlet and enjoy exploring the frozen vly below it, usually a photogenic spot in winter. Then follow the snowmobile trail back to your start on NY 10.

Of course, you must be adept at using a map and compass for the bushwhack route described. Nine Corner Lake lies in a band of extremely heavy winter snows. Snow of great depth, often over four feet, persists through March, so a snowshoe trek is still possible here when the weather becomes a little milder, precluding trips elsewhere.

Stoner Lake Outlet

53 Stoner Lake Outlet

Picnicking

There are several picnic spots of real beauty along NY 10 on the outlet of Stoner Lake. At the first, 1 mile north of Pine Lake, cardinal flowers bloom in August beside the stream, not 50 feet from the road. Opposite the trailhead for Broomstick Lake there is a parking place beside the stream and room for both picnicking and camping.

The best place of all is the Stoner Lake Gorge, 2.5 miles north of Pine Lake. Stretching for 0.2 mile below the outlet of East Stoner Lake, the seemingly remote beauty of the spot belies its proximity to the road. For those who cannot trek to distant gorges, there is no more beautiful place. A series of small falls and deep ledges make it an artist's delight. It is an especially deep, cool, and dark place on a warm sunlit day. In fact, it is so dark it will frustrate photographers, who will find early spring the only time when the gorge is well lighted.

The Stoner Lakes, originally called Stink Lakes in Nick Stoner's time, have various names. West Stoner is consistently called that, but East Stoner was named Middle Stoner on the 1901 Series USGS, when the lake we call Upper Stoner was named East Stoner.

54 West Stoner Lake to Good Luck Lake

Cross-country skiing
2 miles, 1 hour, relatively level, but with lots of minor ups and downs

The route from West Stoner Lake to Good Luck Lake has the distinction of being called the "military road" by some area residents, who believed that it served as a martial route in some war. It certainly was a logging road and at one time part of the principal route north, but no evidence of its military significance has ever been found.

The route has been marked as a snowmobile trail and gives access to several interesting loops. The trail, though sometimes wet, has enough variety to attract summer hikers; however, it is a great ski route. To find the southern end of the trail, drive west from NY 10 along the North Shore Road of West Stoner Lake for almost a mile. That road is the last dirt road on the west before reaching the county line.

The trail heads north from the North Shore Road, following the valley between West Lake Mountain and Rooster Hill, but staying on the east, Rooster Hill, side of that valley. The trail crosses the marked NY 10-Third Lake snowmobile trail, section 56, in just 0.6 mile. Natives call this intersection the "four corners." Continue straight across. In the next 1.4 miles the path is up and down and occasionally wet, crossing four streams before intersecting the Good Luck Lake—Spectacle Lake snowmobile trail 0.3 mile from the southwest corner of Good Luck Lake.

Again continuing straight beyond the connection, the trail skirts the vlies that lie southeast of Good Luck Lake between the water and the road. Unfortunately, the trail isn't close enough to afford interesting summer views. However, because the route follows an old logging road, the grades are relatively gentle with the exception of some steep pitches between four corners and Good Luck Lake. Still, it is perfect for cross-country skiing, with a few pitches between Four Corners and Good Luck Lake.

Use this route for ski-touring practice, returning when you have had enough. Or you could use this route to shorten the trip to Third and Fourth lakes, section 56, or to make an extended trek to Spectacle Lake, section 71. Alternatively, you could use this route for a through-trek across Good Luck Lake. To do this alternative, you will turn right when you reach the Good Luck Lake-Spectacle Lake trail, ski downhill after you reach the level of the lake, and then cut cross-country through the trees, carefully. The open ski trek across the lake to NY 10 can be most attractive, though it is best to stay west of the outlet and on the west side of the West Branch unless that river is securely frozen.

Good Luck Lake

55 Northeast Corner of Jerseyfield
Historical exploration

West Stoner Lake, which lies just south of the Fulton/Hamilton county line, is the site of an easily investigated, though complex, survey situation. The first north line of the present Jerseyfield Patent, run in 1768 in Sir William Johnson's day, met a corner in the "middle" of West Stoner Lake. Two subsequent "corrected" lines (1769/1793) intersected at a "spruce-tree corner," later marked in Verplanck Colvin's day (1883) with a sunken, flat-topped boulder. This is found a few feet north of North Shore West Stoner Lake Road and about 20 feet east of where the trail from Good Luck Lake meets the road, section 54. Benchmark No. 188 is next to the Colvin monument. Going 500 feet at 260° magnetic, passing a mobile home and entering the woods beyond, brings you to a low square stone monument with benchmark No. 88 on top. This is the east end of a long Fulton/Hamilton line-segment relocated in 1926. About 900 feet farther on the 260° bearing, and following occasional yellow paint daubs, brings you to a low rock-cairn, surrounded by yellow-marked witness-trees; this is where the line you are following crosses the original "Indian" line of 1768.

Returning to the "spruce-tree corner" and proceeding 300 feet in the opposite direction, 80° magnetic, brings you to another rock cairn, the east end of the Brayhouse Line of 1806, see section 4.

All four of these corners, by one definition or another, have been the "NE-Corner of Jerseyfield." The stone monument with Benchmark No. 88 is the presently accepted corner. Beside these four, there are four more not so easy to locate, including the original corner in the lake.

56 From NY 10 to Third and Fourth Lakes
Cross-country skiing, hiking
2.8 miles, 1½ hours, relatively level

Third and Fourth lakes used to be accessible from NY 10 entirely by way of an old logging road. The first section of road crosses private lands, however, so when the route was designated a marked snowmobile trail, a new section was cut from NY 10. It intersects the old logging road after 0.2 mile. The trail begins on the west side of NY 10 in Arietta, almost 1 mile north of the Hamilton-Fulton County line. The new section is so wet—parts are under nearly a foot of water sometimes—that the best use of the trail is in winter. Even the snowmobilers avoid this, preferring the old route. Note that all trails in this vicinity are maintained by local groups and establishments and the signs point to Lake's or Avery's—destinations that are bars and restaurants, not natural features.

However, if it is not too wet to walk the first 0.2 mile, the trail does provide hikers a gentle uphill route to Third Lake. If it is too wet, use the first 0.6 mile of the trail north from Stoner Lake to the Four Corners, shortening the route by 0.9 mile. Even the longer route can be covered in an hour and a half. The first part of the trail is through abandoned farmland and woods that have regrown into a dense stand of short, scrubby balsam and spruce trees.

After rising gently to climb around the lower northwest slopes of Rooster Hill, the trail crosses the West Stoner Lake-Good Luck Lake snowmobile trail, section 54, almost 1.5 miles from NY 10. West of the intersection, across the north slopes of West Lake Mountain, the woods are high, open hardwoods with an occasional very large hemlock or spruce. Beyond West Lake Mountain the forest cover again becomes smaller, indicating heavy and more recent logging. Here the trail runs level for nearly 1 mile, over a stretch that is very wet, buggy, and swampy, even in dry weather.

The official marked snowmobile trail reaches the southwest corner of Third Lake near a huge beaver house. In winter snowmobilers continue across the lake to intersect the snowmobile trail from NY 29A along Burnt Vly, section 43.

The old logging road, marked as the trail, does continue for 0.5 mile along the south shore of Third Lake, and although it can be brushy and wet in summer, it is easy to follow to a bridge over the outlet from Fourth Lake into Third Lake. This point in a clearing is north of the old settlement that spanned the outlet closer to Fourth Lake. The settlement today is mostly evident by its huge garbage dump.

Depending on beaver work, you can walk through the clearing and around swampy ground to Fourth Lake on the south. Fourth Lake is almost a carbon copy of Third. Both are 0.5 mile long, rather narrow, swampy at the edges, and surrounded by high ground covered with heavily logged mixed forests. Neither has good views of any of the Adirondacks' high hills.

From the bridge it is 0.2 mile southwest to the intersection with the trail from NY 29A. If you hike to the settlement from NY 10 and return, the round trip will take four hours. Like all the snowmobile trails in the area, this is an excellent cross-country ski route. The snowmobile use is heavy enough to groom the trail for skiers, light enough so that skiers can safely dodge them. As with other abandoned logging roads in the area, this is an ideal route in winter, the lake shores are accessible then and even the trail seems more handsome.

57 Cliffs on Rooster Hill
Easy bushwhack, snowshoeing

Rooster Hill rises to the north of West Stoner Lake. There are no paths on it, but it is easy to bushwhack from NY 10 up along its gentle eastern shoulder to some south-facing cliffs. The views south of distant hills are best in winter. Of course you should be able to read a map and use a compass, but the bushwhack route is rather easy to follow.

Start at the parking turnout on the east side of NY 10 at the north end of East Stoner Lake. Across the road from it and 100 yards north, take a due westerly course for the summit of Rooster Hill. The climb, under 500 feet in over 0.5 mile, is fairly constant. When you reach the summit, walk southwest 300 yards to find the cliffs.

You will be surprised at the depth of the snow on the summit. If you poke about, you may discover other openings with views to the east and southeast, but the views from the cliffs are best. There are no high hills to the immediate south, so the cliffs offer a fine view of distant hills across the Stoner Lakes. The climb takes little more than an hour and a quarter, the return even less.

58 Upper Stoner Lake
Path, picnic spot, walking, fishing, canoeing, camping

The northernmost lake of the three Stoner lakes lies east of NY 10 and is much smaller than either East or West Stoner. It is surrounded entirely by public land and there is easy access to its lovely shores, making it one of the prettiest picnic and camping spots along NY 10.

Park at the turnout at the north end of East Stoner Lake and walk 300 feet along the road. Here a faint footpath heads toward the outlet of Upper Stoner Lake and crosses it. For hikers this crossing can be a wet business of hopping on logs and stones. East of the stream, the path divides; the right or south fork approaches the northern shore of East Stoner Lake. The left fork follows the outlet north a short distance to the southern end of Upper Stoner Lake and a well-used picnic site on a sandy shore under a lovely hemlock grove.

This is an excellent place to bring a rubber boat or a canoe, since the carry is almost nothing. There is another path, but no parking place, on NY 10, just 300 yards north of the marked footpath. This route brings you to the shores of the lake in a few feet, so it is an ideal spot for launching.

There is also a very good path from the picnic site along the southern end of the lake. It runs through a large hemlock stand and leads beside a sphagnum marsh near the lake's inlet. It is amazing that these giants could have survived the tanbark stripping of the nineteenth century or that they could have grown to such a size since then.

Many lovely large birch grace the woods around the lake, and the woods floor, softly cushioned with hemlock needles, is full of many deep woods wild flowers.

59 Brown Lake
Bushwhack

Walk along the south shore of Upper Stoner Lake, following the informal path. Just before it reaches the sphagnum bog, it turns east, staying south of the beautiful, deep moist woods at the eastern edge of the lake. Hunters have kept the route open with notched trees, but at present the path is pretty overgrown. The path heads east northeast through a valley, with the Upper Stoner Lake Inlet to the left, north. After 0.3 mile, the path crosses an intermittent tributary stream, and blazes on the right mark the

Upper Stoner Lake Outlet

beginning of a hunter's route that follows the stream.

At one time a path was blazed that headed southeast about 0.5 mile from Stoner Lake. It circled below a rocky ridge and through an area of blowdowns, then turned northeast, then east across a draw between two small hills, before finally descending to Whitman Flow. This path is no longer discernible.

The path to Brown Lake follows the path above as far as the intermittent stream crossing. Across the stream, continue north-northeast, following the south side of Upper Stoner Lake inlet. At 0.5 mile, the path crosses the inlet and follows its left side until both path and stream (which may dry up altogether in summer) seem to peter out. Continue on a compass course of 45° magnetic beyond the end of the draw. The route will take you through a deep, mossy, heavily wooded hemlock grove. Climb, still on the same compass course, keeping high ground to your right. Bear a little north to go over the tongue of the hill and drop down, still on the compass bearing, to Brown Lake.

The lake is small with steep, wooded shores and two large beaver lodges. You will not find a rock from which to view the lake, but there are several dry wooded places to picnic and a spot on the south shore near the outlet where people have camped. For the return, reversing your compass course will take you back to the well-defined valley that drains into Upper Stoner Lake. Note that the bushwhack is not easy and requires experience with map and compass routes.

60 Hidden Vly
Bushwhack

A lovely, long vly fills the high valley east of East Stoner Lake. The valley drains north into Whitman Flow. A chain of dry meadows leads south from it. To find it, park in the southeast corner of East Stoner Lake where an old road heads into the woods. Follow this roadway for 0.2 mile; the road, which can be skied in winter, heads northeast on high ground, then curves east. For this trek you will walk a path that meets the old road in another mile. For this trek, leave the roadway at 0.2 mile, cross a tiny stream, and discover a small stream.

A narrow path climbs steeply on the southeast bank of the stream. It is a handsome route. The path and the roadway, which is now very faint, rejoin near the height-of-land. The roadway, or the path along it, swings southeast over a small rise, then heads east toward the vly.

This hidden vly extends south for 0.5 mile or so through the high upland valley. Marshes and fields are broken by stretches of woods.

In the days when this was logged, the old roadway continued east to cross Whitman Flow. Hunters kept open a trail that extended from it up to the high plateau north of Shaker Mountain. The path once led to Duck Lake. A shorter approach to this area is from Pinnacle Road, section 81. If you are the kind of bushwhacker who needs no more help than your map and compass, you can tackle the route. Directions for this bushwhack are omitted as it is much too difficult for the average hiker.

Headwaters of the West Branch of the Sacandaga

WEST BRANCH COUNTRY is true wilderness, perhaps the southern Adirondacks' least-known area. It is the heart of the Silver Lake Wilderness Area, so no motorized vehicles are permitted east of NY 10, keeping it remote and unspoiled. Half the forest covered in this book lies within the circle of the West Branch of the Sacandaga River, and the few accesses to it keep it largely untouched for those adventurous individuals who like to bushwhack. Though many of its forests were logged in the nineteenth century, they have had nearly a century to recover. Logging was mostly selective and never severe. This combined with the deep, rich soils and the lower elevation makes the forests among the most majestic in the Adirondacks. Thus, this area fulfills the ideals of true wilderness in a way no other Adirondack area so designated is able to do.

The West Branch of the Sacandaga, frequently changing its mood and tempo, flows in every direction around the compass. Arising in three small streams from three small lakes in deep forest, the river winds like a spiral as if to protect its interior from intruders. The West Branch flows south and west from Meco Lake and near the Whitman Flow joins the outlet of Silver Lake, which has already made its way southward for 4 miles. Together they flow west to pick up the North Branch, which has come nearly 6 miles south from Canary Pond.

Meandering west 4 miles to NY 10, which crosses it twice in the space of 1 mile, the river then turns north to wander leisurely for 6 miles through a majestic valley. As the road parallels the river here, it can be enjoyed easily at many places by hikers as well as by canoe.

Located on NY 10 on a large piece of private land in the midst of the Forest Preserve is Avery's Hotel, a typical old Adirondack hotel and hunting lodge that even boasts a private lake and game preserve stocked with many deer. The view from its porch across the valley of the West Branch, where it winds and twists through a broad meadow, is as spectacular as any in the southern Adirondacks. Flowing through the longest and highest

West Branch of the Sacandaga River

of the mountain valleys, the river has cut a sinuous path through the silted plain left when a glacial lake receded.

North of Avery's, the river bends to the east past the site of an old Shaker farm, which now is little more than a sand pit. Then falling through the first of a great series of rapids, it continues northeast to pick up the outlet of Piseco Lake in another quiet stretch.

Their union is far from quiet, for as the river turns again, now to the east, it becomes a raging stream. Tumbling east for 14 miles over cataracts, rapids, and falls, it drops nearly 700 feet. One stretch has been designated a Wild River in the New York State Wild, Scenic and Recreational Rivers System. From Piseco Outlet east to the quiet of Big Eddy near Whitehouse, West Branch country is as remote and inaccessible as any part of our wild Adirondacks. Known only to hunters and trappers and a few fishermen, this section has an incomparable beauty.

East of Whitehouse, the site of an old hunting lodge that is now part of the Forest Preserve, the river is within reach of a dirt road that remains the only intrusion of civilization into the region. Here the rapids widen into a wide, rocky, river bed, innocuous enough in summer, but deep and violent with spring rains.

Below Wells, the river turns again, once more heading south to join the Main Branch of the Sacandaga. This river continues south to pass scarcely 7 miles as the crow flies from the headwaters of the West Branch, thus almost encircling its wilderness interior. Because NY 30 is east of the river, with bridges only at Wells and near Benson, the river is here as much a barrier to the woods it borders as are the posted private lands that edge the encircling roads.

NY 10, the only access to the western part of West Branch territory, is now a smooth, curving, two-lane highway, where just a few years ago it was only a bumpy gravel road. But the new road maintains a measure of the wilderness route; a constitutional amendment, which would have permitted a straightened superhighway through this portion of the Adirondack Park, was fortunately defeated.

Just north of Arietta, where NY 10 crosses the West Branch twice, the "two bridge area" holds a special fascination because of the numerous paths that explore it. But it also has a special problem, for here the different scales of the USGS topographical maps are most confusing to hikers. Out of habit, the easternnmost bridge north of Arietta is called the first bridge and the western one the second. Although the river is generally flowing north to south beside NY 10, it briefly flows east to west in the vicinity of the bridges.

West Branch of the Sacandaga River

61 West Branch of the Sacandaga/Upstream from the First Bridge

Canoeing

While canoeing the West Branch upstream from the first bridge north of Arietta is difficult, it permits you to penetrate some of the most inaccessible parts of West Branch country. Park at the first bridge 1.7 miles north of the Hamilton-Fulton county line on NY 10.

Low water could hamper this trip, but so could a cold, wet day with unusually high water and heavy current. The greatest impediment occurs right at the start, for there are rapids for the first 0.2 mile. Line (drag with a rope) your canoe while walking beside the stream because the path beside the river, section 63, is so overgrown in summer that portaging along it can be difficult. From the head of these rapids upstream to the east, there is a lovely stretch of calm water. At 1 mile a small stream enters from the north; it is the North Branch where at one time a huge beaver dam impounded a fairly large pond.

You have to drag your canoe over many small beaver dams on the way

Map V: Sections 61-69, 77-78, 83-85, 87, 97, 99

Based on UGGS Piseco Lake and Lake Pleasant 15' Quadrangles

— — — Trail

—·—·— Path

· · · · · Bushwhack

Canoe Route

——— Road

Overlook

Shelter

upstream on the West Branch. With a few carries, the West Branch is navigable for 3 miles east of the rapids. The river winds through grassy meadows, occasionally close to the heavily wooded southern shore. Silver Lake Outlet flows in from the northwest at the end of the floatable stream; then, in a big bend, White Lake Outlet joins from the north and Whitman Flow from the south. The West Branch swings northeast and continues with steep shores through nearly a mile of rapids. An upstream section of nearly 2 miles is canoeable, but virtually inaccessible.

Round trip to the rapids below Silver Lake Outlet takes about five hours. However, a long portage awaits you if you want to travel further. On foot, you can walk east, cutting across high ground to the head of the rapids, where a deceptive widening proves not to be the big flows. East of the widening, cross to the south side as the river here plunges through a steep gorge and you will be obliged to walk high above the river in the woods. Upstream from the gorge, the river finally widens into flows, which stretch for nearly 2 miles. The longest canoeable stretch is created by a beaver dam that is more than five feet high and a hundred feet wide.

√ 62 West Branch of the Sacandaga/ Downstream from the First Bridge

Canoeing

Hamilton County is fortunate in having several long canoeable waterways with high starting elevations, some of which are the most accessible in the Adirondacks. The favorite flat water trip is along the West Branch as it meanders northward through a wide meadow with excellent views of surrounding mountains.

The river winds through the valley from the first bridge to Shaker Place, taking such a sinuous course that the canoeable stream exceeds 10 miles in length, although the distances the crow flies is but 6 miles. With a slight current, barely enough to help the paddler, it is a leisurely way to enjoy nature. The infrequent small beaver dams that require portaging scarcely obstruct the gentle route. Allow between four and five hours for the one-way trip.

The starting elevation is 1660 feet, unusually high for such a long, flat stream. The trip can be made in any water level, but a cool summer day with wind is preferable because spring bugs in the swamp can be fierce. However, the entire stream is lovely at any time of year. In early summer swarms of butterflies, fritillaries, and red admirals play over the tall grasses and milkweed along the stream. Occasionally deer show themselves, and in early August a few cardinal flowers dot the banks and sometimes fields of Joe-Pye weed turn the horizon pink. Late in summer and in early fall, swamp maples and witch hobble make the shoreline a magenta ribbon.

The trip begins at the first bridge. Spot a car at Shaker Place, nearly 8 miles north, where a road leads into the sand pit that fills the fields at Shaker Place. The road is not usually barred so you can drive right to the bank of the West Branch, either close to NY 10 or 200 yards downstream at the ruins of an old dam and bridge at the head of the rapids that mark the end of this canoe trip.

NY 10 follows the entire route, but you will rarely be aware of its existence. Note that you can shorten the trip by starting by the second bridge or at one of several points farther north. One alternate is 0.7 mile north of the second bridge, near the flow created by State Brook, which is very narrow and shallow, but navigable. Put your canoe in on the east side; the West Branch is but 100 yards away. Another possible beginning, 1.2 miles north of the second bridge, requires a carry of about 100 yards. Here in the vicinity of Trout Lake, a path leads from the highway toward the river. Perhaps one of the greatest charms of the West Branch is that you do not have to canoe it all at once, for there are enough launching spots to break the trip into leisurely segments.

Between the first and second bridge, 1.2 miles by road, the stream flows almost due west with a few obstructions. The stream approaches the road, then turns away from it to be joined by the small outlet of Good Luck Lake, which is almost hidden in the brushy marsh. This is your first introduction to the West Branch's second charm, the many excursions from the main stream that lead to other lakes and streams. Use the outlet to reach the lake and canoe to one of the lake's campsites, section 70.

The river turns north, crossing under the second bridge, and 0.2 mile from the bridge, the river angles west. Here the outlet of Chub Lake flows in from the right, or east. If beaver have been active, the outlet may be navigable. Often, however, the 0.2-mile side channel is too shallow and the sides too boggy to walk along to line a canoe.

Farther downstream, the course of the river is generally north through the valley between State Brook Mountain on the west and Trout Lake Mountain on the east. State Brook comes in from the west in this section, although its entrance is scarcely noticeable in the main river's many twists, turns, and backwaters.

If you want an adventurous side trip, look carefully along the north bank of the West Branch, about 200 yards upstream from the confluence of State Brook. The place is in the midst of a huge swampy meadow without good landmarks. A small stream enters from the east. It does not appear to be navigable, for there are scarcely two inches of water near the confluence in summer. However, beaver have created a series of ponds upstream behind a row of dams, none of which are more than a foot high. The first, fortunately, is only 100 feet from the confluence. If the series of dams holds, you can canoe for 0.5 mile to the east. This unnamed stream drains the valley between Sherman and Chub Lake mountains. There are fields of weathered stumps and twisted roots and logs, accessible only by water. The reflections and images of mountains, sky, and sculptured wooden forms makes this one of the best side trips along the West Branch.

Nearly 2 miles downstream from the second bridge, Trout Lake flows in from the east. The excursion to Trout Lake is lovely, and if water is high enough, you can continue to the northeast to the end of shallow Little Trout Lake, not quite 2 miles round trip. The more distant pond (these are really shallow bodies of water) boasts a huge beaver lodge on its northern shore. If you look southeast from the northern end of the pond, you will have a fine view of the northwest side of the cliffs on Sherman Mountain, section 67.

Nick Stoner built one of his bark cabins on the bank of the West Branch by the outlet of Trout Lake. He stayed there when he was setting traps for beaver along the river. This site, according to his biographer, Simms, in *Trappers of New York*, was the spot where two St. Regis Indians attempted to steal pelts and traps from Stoner. Needless to say, the great trapper dispatched the Indians, but the tale is worth reading before you canoe the river. Actually, several chapters of that biography deal with Stoner's adventures along the West Branch and serve as a good introduction to the area.

Returning to the river and again heading north, downstream, you may be surprised to see cars on NY 10, but this view lasts but a moment as the river again turns. Its corkscrew route will almost turn back upon itself so that many minutes of paddling often yield no real progress through the valley.

About 6 miles from the start, the stream begins a slow meander through the broad flowed lands to the east of Avery's Hotel. South of here, there have been a few camps along the stream, and north of Avery's, where the river winds around Pine Mountain, there is still some private land. Further north the shores are mostly state owned. There is but one reminder of civilization—a few logs from the old logging bridge west of Pine Mountain. It is so collapsed that it is no longer necessary to carry a canoe over it. Beyond is a stretch recently acquired by the state.

The entire river is a haven for many birds. In the northern flows marsh hawks perch right above the river. Olive-sided fly-catchers and rose-breasted grosbeaks flock in the trees beside the river and hummingbirds mass in the flowers below. Red admiral butterflies join painted ladies and tortoise shell butterflies in the fields beside the banks. If you are very observant, you will notice that the white admiral butterfly appears in both this northern form and the southern red spotted purple and in hybrids of the two, for this area lies in the band of hybridization. Even if you are not adept at recognizing butterflies, you will enjoy the dragon flies and bottle flies flashing every iridescent shade imaginable as they light on your canoe.

Toward the end of the trip, just before rough water, you will arrive at the site of a long deserted farm settled by Shakers, who began the manufacture of barrel staves and baker's peels and lived at the West Branch site for less than a decade in the early 1800s. Even their fields have been excavated, leaving only a sand pit. The Shaker Place continued as a farmsite for many years, and from 1870 to 1900 it was the center of a large logging operation. A dam at Shaker Place impounded water for the spring run of logs, flooding much of the West Branch Valley. The entire valley was once a long, glacial lake, and the present river has carved its sinuous course through the sandy deposits laid down by the glaciers.

With a car at either end, you can easily make the through trip in one day and include most of the excursions. If you want to turn it into a two day, overnight camping trip, note that good, dry campsites are not numerous because of the extent of the flowed lands bordering the river. The best overnight spots are on the hill northwest of Pine Mountain or on the high shores of the connected lakes: Good Luck, Chub, and Trout.

63 North Branch Reservoir

Path and bushwhack, hiking, cross-country skiing, snowshoeing, fishing, camping

A logging road penetrated nearly 5 miles northeast into the wilderness from the first bridge over the West Branch of the Sacandaga. That road was actively used during the last half of the nineteenth century. Today a walk along paths that follow its course is an adventure into a primitive and massively timbered country with lovely and varied water views.

Like most good paths in West Branch Country, the most accessible, and in this case the southern portion, has been kept open by sportsmen. At its far northern end, the logging road has become so overgrown and difficult to follow that it must be considered a bushwhack.

The roadway began on the northeast corner of the first bridge on NY 10, north of Arietta, right beside the modern parking turnout. At present, it is marked only by a narrow footpath through the open field that in summer is filled with bedstraw, goldenrod, asters, and blackberries, covering the way and often growing higher than the average hiker's head. In spring, before the tangle of plants has had time to grow, the path is more obvious and is well used by fishermen.

This rank growth has for years hidden an archeological treasure. In the 1870s a tannery occupied the field beside the river. Stone foundations from the long buildings can be found right beside the path. However, you would be wise to look for them in earliest spring, for they lie in tangled underbrush and thickets of new trees. In spring you can trace out rows of several buildings and find a wall, standing over two stories high, nestled against the hillside. You may even be able to find the exit flume through which acid wastes of the tannery were flushed back into the river. Pottery pieces, rusted cans and pipes, tea kettles, and hinges are all concealed in the weeds. Foundations can be found 100 feet from the highway and for 300 yards along the river. Two hundred men worked here, cutting hemlock, peeling bark, and grinding it to prepare the tanning liquor used to cure skins brought from all over the East. The tannery closed by 1880. Searching out its remains deserves several hours of exploration, probably more than can be combined with a trip to the North Branch Reservoir.

About 0.3 mile from the start, the path swings north away from the river around a large swampy area. The beaver swamp that caused this detour is drying, so that fishermen have pushed a path closer to the river.

After swinging north around the swamp, the path heads southeast toward the area where the North Branch flows into the West Branch. A thirty-minute walk from NY 10, the trail angles northeast to follow the North Branch quite closely on a bank above it, though you will not often see or hear it. Several old beaver dams cross the stream in an area of quiet flow. The path comes out in a small meadow, 2 miles from the start. This meadow borders still another beaver flow created by a long dam, but the pond upstream is well below the level the dam once held. The beaver flow is near the site of a house that served the caretaker of the Arietta Game Preserve. The foundations and root cellar, dug by Bill Hunter, are still there. The meadow, which has a few old apple trees, is a lovely picnic site and is occasionally used by sportsmen as a campsite.

The game preserve was one of a series of steps taken by the state in the late 1920s to improve deer herds. After logging ceased at the turn of the century, open areas created unusually good forage areas for deer, and the deer herds became exceptionally large. With the rapid recovery of the southern Adirondack forests and increased hunting pressure the deer herd was again limited. The preserve, built in 1927 was an abortive attempt to increase the herd. A single strand of wire surrounded nearly 4000 acres of Forest Preserve, along the county line, then north past White Lake and west to NY 10.

At the cabin foundation in the woods, west of the meadow, the old roadway makes a right-angle turn to the left, then bends right, heading due north and briefly away from the stream. After passing through a thick hemlock stand, it again swings quite close to the stream at the point where the stream makes a large bend. Here the path forks with the right branch approaching the stream and the left one heading just a little west of north around a hairpin loop in the North Branch. This is the closest the path approaches the river between the meadow and an area 1.5 miles north.

In the vicinity of the fork and again 0.5 mile farther north where the path bends east, the roadway has become increasingly difficult to discern. Beyond the meadow hikers should notice a dramatic change in the character of the land, for the stream is now east of Sherman Mountain and at least 3 miles from any roads, so it has always been remote and inaccessible. There are still signs that the path follows an old road, but the trees are of such enormous size that it seems as if none of the area was ever logged. Birch and maple of such proportions might be expected, but the size of softwoods is astounding. Probably only the tanbarkers ventured this far, and large hemlock with a heavy coating of mosses replacing their stripped barks still lie near the path. However, many large hemlock remain growing.

The path follows the stream north, staying a couple hundred yards west of it. It is necessary to leave the path and bushwhack east to see this section that alternates between stretches of small rapids and long peaceful flows. Look carefully for the place 1.5 miles north of the Game Preserve headquarters where the path again comes quite close to the North Branch. Here, there is a beaver flow downstream and a rocky section upstream, so it is possible to hop rocks and cross. The North Branch bends just below the rocky section, and at the northeast corner of the curve, a very small stream enters from the east. If you follow it for less than 0.2 mile you will come to Ross Lake, a narrow body of water rimmed on the south with small cliffs.

Back on the old road bed, you can tell that a section 0.5 mile farther north was at one time flooded by a beaver pond. The roadway is only a few feet from the abandoned beaver house and almost impossible to discern.

The path becomes increasingly difficult to follow. Old maps indicate that the road stopped at the next meadow, which is surprising in light of the rock work farther north. It is difficult to follow the river here, but a short trek, 200 yards north through thick brush, leads to the waterfall on the North Branch. The twelve-foot fall tumbles into a deep pool whose western edge was lined with a rock diversion wall to steer logs down the river. The flat rocks above the fall make a good place to stop and rest and picnic.

Above the fall you can see the remains of a small stone dam. Skirting the meadow above the first dam can be difficult, but above the remains of the second dam, a long dry meadow stretches north for 1.5 miles. The North Branch now meanders through this meadow as a quiet-flowing stream. However, the amount of water that could be impounded makes it possible to believe that there was enough to float logs to the old mill on NY 10, some 5.5 miles away. Trout fishing was once considered exceptionally fine in the old reservoir, and it still may be because the falls provide a natural barrier against warm-water species that inhabit the river downstream.

You can walk north along the meadow through the dry reservoir which is dominated on the west by North Branch Mountain. At the north end of the meadow the North Branch forks. The east fork is the outlet of Canary Pond. It can be used as a guide for a 1-mile bushwhack route northeast to Canary Pond to pick up the Northville-Placid Trail.

The round trip walk to the reservoir takes a full day. There are endless camping spots along the way. In winter snowshoe or cross-country ski trips to the North Branch Reservoir are possible, either along the path or on the frozen flows.

64 Silver Lake Outlet
Bushwhack

In order to reach and walk along the path that follows an abandoned road beside Silver Lake Outlet, you first have to trek nearly 1.5 miles from NY 10 along the beginning of the old road described in section 63. Then you have to walk 2 miles on a faint road between the North Branch and Silver Lake Outlet. The path along Silver Lake Outlet is just as desirable as the one beside the North Branch, for it is equally remote, and subtle differences make it a completely different experience.

The walk can take over four and a half hours, much of which is required for the round trip to the point where Silver Lake Outlet flows into the West Branch.

Begin as for the path to the North Branch Reservoir. At 0.3 mile, where the path begins to swing north, keep to the path that follows the river more closely. Recent drying of the swamp makes this possible, though you will have to cross one stream. If you take the arc to the north around the swamp, watch at 1.5 miles for a fork where a path heads off to the south. The path intersects the more direct route in only 50 feet and heads southeast to the confluence of the North and West branches. High grass usually obscures the area just before you reach the confluence. In low water, jump across the North Branch; in high water, you have to wade across.

Continuing mileages are given from the confluence. You may have to search about for the path on the east side. It enters a softwood thicket, bisecting the angle between the two streams. A quarter mile past the confluence, the path angles north around a swampy place. You must search for the continuing path that angles south. At the end of this stretch, the path reaches a huge swamp formed by an old, long, curved, and partly overgrown beaver dam that is about 20 feet to the right of the path's apparent end. Cross the dam and look to the right for the path, which will still serve to lead you east; in fact, it becomes much more open and easy to follow than at the beginning.

The path enters a dry meadow at just short of 2 miles from the confluence. It is easy to traverse the meadow if you keep to its northern side. You reach the West Branch and Silver Lake Outlet at the eastern end of the meadow. Turn north, within sight of the stream, to follow the narrow but visible footpath that parallels the outlet north for 1.2 miles. Of course, it is possible to follow the stream north beyond the point the path disappears.

The steep mountain to the east and the beautiful stream make this the most pleasant part of the walk. There are several small islands, heavily wooded, in the southern quiet part of the stream, but farther north, where the outlet is narrower and rocky, it tumbles nearly 200 feet through a deep gorge beside White Lake Mountain. It is a rare pleasure to follow the path until it disappears along the small cascades of this remote and unspoiled stream.

65 Chub Lake
Path, walking, canoeing, snowshoeing

Chub Lake is one of the easiest bogs to reach and explore in the southern Adirondacks. It lies on the north side of NY 10 between the two bridges over the West Branch. There is a good but unmarked path to it from the road, 5.8 miles north of Pine Lake, less than 1 mile north of the first bridge and 0.1 mile east of the parking turnout between the bridges.

By a sign indicating a sharp turn, drop down the bank beside the road and step into a deep, moist woods. The path, about 0.15 mile long, leads directly to the lake and an informal path continues along the shore to the east, right.

The quaking bog itself, which lies mostly on the east and north sides of the lake, is composed of thick layers of sphagnum moss upon which grow wild cranberries; bog rosemary; two insectivorous plants, the pitcher plant and sundew; and two native orchids, the grass pink and rose pogonia. Perhaps you will spot a small grey butterfly, the bog copper, which is found only in swamps. Chub Lake has both yellow and purple bladderwort, pale blue lobelia, bog wool, and the fairy-like stalks of swamp candles. The swampy borders house a profusion of woody plants such as bog rosemary, sheep laurel, tamarack, and swamp maples.

A large rock stands out on the northeast shore; it is a good picnic spot. An informal path around the south and east end of the lake leads beside some of the sphagnum mats and eventually arrives at the rock. Because the access path is so short, it is easy to carry a canoe in for exploring the boggy shores.

Wear rubber boots or old sneakers and plan on getting wet if you chose to challenge the support of the layers of sphagnum in an attempt to reach the tiny bog plants. Do walk carefully so as not to disturb them or step through a hole in the bog. And, do not forget a camera and a wildflower identification book.

Chub Lake Mountain lies east of the lake and the cliffs near its summit offer a limited view of the surrounding mountains, among them Good Luck, State Brook, and Sherman. A bushwhack of little more than 0.5 mile and a half-hour's walk from NY 10 leads to these cliffs. Start on the path to the lake, walk east around it, leaving the informal path where it turns north. Bushwhack east or just a little north of east. This way you will be walking with the cliffs on your left or north, but you will be climbing almost the steepest and most direct route to the summit of the small hill. The cliffs are just below the summit and to its west.

66 The Upper Cliffs on Sherman Mountain
Bushwhack, snowshoeing

As you drive north from Pine Lake along NY 10, you will see a handsome meadow on the north side of the road within sight of the second bridge over the West Branch. Stop here and study the two mountains to the north and northeast; they are the focus for four difficult bushwhacks that offer the best snowshoe trips in the area. All require knowledge of the use of map and compass, and each is a full-day outing.

View from Sherman Mountain

Northeast of the meadow, across Chub Lake, you can see Sherman Mountain. Its upper cliffs are clearly defined on the southwest face of the summit. A second set of cliffs, lower and farther west, is hidden from view. The upper cliffs offer a lovely view of the West Branch valley. When you view the cliffs from NY 10, do not let their apparent closeness deceive you. They are over 1.5 miles away as the crow flies, and the approach is through rugged terrain. The cliffs are just below the summit, which at 2640 feet in elevation is almost 1000 feet above the West Branch Valley. This bushwhack route to the cliffs is almost the shortest and easiest route, and it manages to pass most of the best features in the immediate vicinity. With time for lunch or photographs, the bushwhack is a good five hour adventure.

Begin as for Chub Lake, crossing the frozen surface of the lake in winter, circling it in summer, to the rock outcrop on the far northeast shore. Enter the woods to the left of the outcrop and continue in a northeasterly direction. You will climb over a small rise and drop into a small valley, which you will follow northeast to the foot of Chub Lake Mountain. The route passes just below its lower cliffs although you will not see the higher portions; in winter their face is hung with great amber-colored icicles.

Continue northeast over a second rise and down into the valley of an unnamed stream flowing from east to west. Walk upstream, crossing to the north side. Choose the point to cross with care, as the stream is usually open in winter. Continue following the stream to the east, watching the contour of the land to the north with care. You should observe two valleys formed by intermittent streams that nearly intersect at the stream you are following. The western one is formed by the foot of the cliffs. You will be looking for the eastern one, however, for it is the best route to the upper cliffs. It is littered with huge boulders and glacial erratics, one of which is a precariously perched balancing rock weighing about fifty tons. It marks a good place to stop for a winter picnic.

Climbing the boulder-filled valley is not easy; the best route is on the east side. A long, level shelf in the mountain face will be your clue to the best way to climb through the cliffs. Follow the level area east to its end and then make a steep 100-foot climb to the shoulder of the mountain. Even though the way seems very steep, this approach to the summit is the most gentle. At the summit, proceed west and back from the spruce thickets that line the cliffs. You will be looking for the one area where the thickets open up enough to provide a view of the valley below. The spot is a cleft in the face of the cliff; from it you can enjoy views of the West Branch Valley with Trout Lake Mountain to the west and Good Luck Lake to the southwest.

From the summit, you should retrace your steps. Do not be tempted to find the lower set of cliffs from here because the cliffs surrounding most of the summit are too steep for safe travel. Save a walk to the lower cliffs for another day.

67 The Lower Cliffs on Sherman Mountain

Bushwhack, snowshoeing

The lower cliffs on Sherman Mountain are also reached by starting the bushwhack from the rock on Chub Lake. A route north-northeast from the rock leads to the valley between Sherman and Trout Lake mountains. Walk up the north side of the valley, keeping back from the edge of the cliffs as they develop. The going is rough near the cliff edges, and the spruce thickets can seem impenetrable. There are two or three places with views, but the best is farther north along the range of cliffs. This vantage has views of Little Trout Lake. This bushwhack is difficult; although the route is shorter both in length and ascent than the one to the upper cliffs, it requires almost as much time to complete the round trip. You will bushwhack over 3 miles and climb 600 feet.

68 Circuit to Trout Lake, below Trout Lake Mountain Cliffs

Bushwhack, snowshoeing

A marvelous winter trip can be devised that brings you past the cliffs on Trout Lake Mountain to Trout Lake and back through the valley between Sherman and Trout Lake Mountains. The end of the trip will take you below the lower cliffs described above, and the beginning will take you by some wonderful ice formations on the face of Trout Lake Mountain.

The route of the trip's beginning is determined by the thickness of the ice in the flow of the unnamed stream north of Chub Lake. With care and good ice, it is possible to go northwest from Chub Lake across a low hemlock-covered promontory to the flow, cut directly across it, and come out under the Trout Lake Mountain cliffs. If ice might be a problem, cross the stream farther east, where it is narrow, and make a longer trek around the south side of Trout Lake Mountain.

The columns of ice on the cliffs take on a rainbow of hues, from yellow

View from Trout Lake Mountain

to blue, and the whole becomes a colorful array of organ pipes. It is easy to snowshoe north, curving around the base of the mountain, to Trout Lake. Continue north over Trout Lake and its flow to Little Trout Lake. You might enjoy the ledge on the northeastern shore of the lake for a picnic. Notice that this is the corner into which the outlet of Lost Pond flows.

From the corner of Little Trout Lake you can either head east-southeast to climb over the lower cliffs on Sherman or make your way into the valley between the two mountains. If you choose the latter, pick your course southeast carefully to find the draw. Climbing into the valley is difficult. Sherman's lower cliffs loom above the saddle of the valley. Descend the valley to the unnamed stream, cross it, and head southwest toward Chub Lake and the return. The trek is at least 5 miles long and requires as many hours. The saddle is only 260 feet above the level of Chub Lake, but it is a stiff climb. While part of the navigating is easy, finding and getting back from the valley between Sherman and Trout Lake mountains is difficult, so you should consider the whole a difficult bushwhack.

69 Trout Lake Mountain Cliffs
Bushwhack, snowshoeing

A climb to the cliffs on Trout Lake Mountain can be made in either winter or summer. In summer, you can choose one of two routes. The easier requires a canoe. Launch on the West Branch at either the second bridge or State Brook, section 62. From either, paddle north, stopping where the river makes its closest approach to dry land below the mountain. The climb from here is very steep, but you should reach the base of the cliffs within half an hour; walk east to climb around behind them to their tops.

The second way is entirely by foot. Walk around Chub Lake as if to climb Sherman's lower cliffs, but after crossing the unnamed stream, head northwest up the long shoulder of Trout Lake Mountain. This route is longer but more gentle than the route from the West Branch landing spot. The 2-mile bushwhack and climb will take about two hours. The cliffs are below and west of the summit, which is almost 600 feet above the West Branch.

The winter trek from Chub Lake is shorter because you can cross the lake directly. Start as if you were walking below Trout Lake Mountain's cliffs. As soon as you cross the stream, head north up the mountain, then angle northwest, across the mountain, and descend to the level of the cliffs. Use caution near the cliff tops!

√ **70** Good Luck Lake

Path, walking, camping, fishing, canoeing, cross-country skiing

Good Luck Lake was named not for any wonderful catch of fish but for an incident that occurred when Lawrence Vrooman was surveying near the lake. According to Jeptha R. Simms, in his *Trappers of New York*, "several of the party were making a large canoe from the trunk of a tree, and John Burgess, his son-in-law, discharged his gun at a loon, off on the water. The piece burst and scattered its fragments harmlessly in every direction. The accident terminated so fortunately that the name the lake now bears was entered on the surveyor's field-book."

Good Luck Lake is easily accessible from NY 10. There are several good camping sites on its northern shore, all high and dry, beneath large pine and hemlock trees. Both the 0.5-mile path into the lake and the short path across its northern shore are good, open walking routes.

Park in the turnout just west of the second bridge above Arietta; the Good Luck Lake path and a snowmobile trail both begin within 100 feet of one another on the south side of the road opposite the turnout. The eastern entrance is the one to Good Luck Lake.

For fifteen or twenty minutes you head almost due south to the lake over the shoulder of a small hill. Several huge, flat-topped stumps along this trail indicate how large trees grew in this area before it was logged, more than fifty years ago. As the path descends to the lake, it splits several ways, all going to different camping sites along the northern shore. The lake is small, only 0.5 mile long, and it is possible to explore its northern shore from the path and enjoy the quiet charm of the lake from several places on that shore.

Most of the upland lakes are more fun when explored by boat, but the arduous portages required to put a canoe on them outweigh the advantages. Good Luck Lake is a delightful exception. And, of course, it is much easier to camp on the north shore if you can bring in a pack by boat. To reach the lake by water, put a canoe in the West Branch beside the second bridge where there is a good launching site. Paddle upstream or south for 300 yards. As the stream heads east, look for the small stream flowing in from the south through a swampy area. Weeds occasionally obscure the stream's mouth; in fact, sometimes it is hardly visible at all. The outlet of Good Luck Lake is narrow but navigable, winding through the swamp with perhaps one or two small portages over the remains of beaver dams, depending on the water level. From the water you will be aware of the significant pines among the hemlock on the north shore. Tamarack fill the swamps on the south and east. The paddle is but 0.5 mile to the lake, and you may see ducks in the weed beds on the southeastern shore.

Section 71 details a longer trail that almost touches the western end of the pond. A bushwhack of 200 yards puts you on the northern shore of Good Luck Lake for a ciruit walk.

√ ## 71 Spectacle Lake

Trail along old road, hiking, camping, fishing, cross-country skiing, snowshoeing
2.8 miles, 1½ hours, relatively level

Spectacle Lake was obviously named for its lobes, which suggest a pair of eyeglasses. However, the first surveyors must have failed to discover all of the lake's circular recesses or else had in mind a many-eyed monster outfitted with a very peculiar pair of spectacles. A deep, evergreen-covered peninsula separates the two largest lobes, and smaller peninsulas and islands define numerous others.

Spectacle's shores are so swampy and difficult to walk through—there is no path around the circumference—that the best way to explore the 1.5-mile-long chain of bays is on skis or snowshoes in winter or from a canoe in summer. In fact, this is perhaps one of the more disappointing lakes for hikers because the shores are so swampy and so little of it can be seen at one time. Other snowmobile routes lead to the lakeshore, section 44, but the only other approach by trail is at the easternmost corner.

With a canoe, though, you can appreciate the quiet water and explore the coves and bays for ducks and loons as well as fish for the warm-water species that inhabit the lake. A lovely series of little falls marks the outlet of Dry Lake into the western lobe of Spectacle. It would be impossible to see if you couldn't paddle to the stream and then walk up along it.

Camping here at the end of a day of canoeing is among the most desirable ways to enjoy this distant lake. The very long, thin peninsula that divides the middle from the eastern lobe is high and dry. Its good evergreen cover shelters the best camping sites on the lake, although there are several other decent spots, including some on the northeast shore of the easternmost lobe.

Because all of the routes to the lake are over 3 miles long, you may wish to use the canoe trip into Good Luck Lake, section 70, to shorten the carry. In that lake, head for the southwest corner, staying just to the east of two small inlet streams there to avoid the swamps. The bushwhack from the shore to the Spectacle Lake snowmobile trail is probably shortest from this spot. Pick a course south-southwest near the stream, crossing it where it bends west, to find the trail. Cutting through the woods this way, a distance of less than 0.2 mile, eliminates over 1.5 miles of trail portaging and brings you to a spot on the trail about 1.5 miles from Spectacle.

The most direct land route to Spectacle Lake is along the snowmobile trail described here. Park at the turnout north of the second bridge on NY 10, the same access for Good Luck Lake. The trail, which follows an old roadbed, is the northernmost of the two entrances opposite the parking turnout. The trail heads west for just under 0.5 mile to a four-way intersection with a trail registration booth. The right fork is marked "Avery's," the route straight ahead goes to Dry and Dexter Lakes, section 72, and your route to Spectacle Lake is the left fork, unofficially marked "Arietta, Pleasant Lake, and Lakes."

Beyond the intersection, the Spectacle Lake trail bears a little west of south for 0.7 mile, passing close enough to Good Luck Lake so that it is visible through the trees. The trail descends to a six-foot bridge over an intermittent stream, then climbs a small rise to descend and cross a second, larger stream on a fifteen to twenty-foot bridge. (Note this is the beginning of the path to Good Luck Cliffs, section 73.)

The snowmobile trail then climbs a small hill and makes a big loop to the west around a swamp, crossing another stream. There is a forty-foot section of planking across the stream in the swamp. The trail swings back east, climbing a small hill. At the intersection at 1.5 miles, the principal route continues uphill and south around Good Luck Lake, leading to West Stoner Lake, section 54. Here a right turn is the beginning of the trail west to Spectacle Lake. This route, considerably narrower, winds about, and enters a draw, headed toward Spectacle Lake.

The trail pursues an up-and-down course over rolling terrain in the last 1.2 mile stretch to the lake. This stretch is quite narrow and twisty and can be difficult to ski. A thick hemlock forest edges the trail. The distance from Good Luck to Spectacle is 1.8 miles, and the total distance from NY 10 is just short of 2.8 miles.

The trail ends at the lakeshore, and there is no sign of the continuing route that at one time followed the southeast shore and connected with the roads that are now the trails to Third and Fourth lakes, section 43.

Generally, the trail along the road bed from NY 10 is well suited to cross-country skiing and is maintained well enough to be recommended, though the hillocks along the trail east of Good Luck Lake offer a little challenge. You can ski the 3-mile distance to the lake in just over an hour. Ski down Spectacle Lake past the two peninsulas and the wooded island to the boulder island in the distant lobe and explore some of the bays there. You will find the giant boulder sitting in the last bay near Dry Lake Outlet. Be sure to look back northeast to the cliffs on Good Luck Mountain. A trip up the lake and back adds a minimum of 3 miles to the trek, so the 9-mile outing this provides is a long day's work if you have to break trail, a four-hour trek if there are tracks to follow. Even on weekends you will probably not meet more than a couple of snowmobiles—and chances are you will have this distant lake all to yourself.

On your return, you would enjoy leaving the Spectacle Lake snowmobile trail at its closest approach to Good Luck Lake. Ski across the lake toward its outlet and follow the northern shore of the outlet and the West Branch back to NY 10, coming out within 100 yards of your car. This variation does not shorten the trip, but it eliminates some climbing and is a pretty addition to the ski trek.

72 Dry and Dexter Lakes, Extension to Western Spectacle Lake

Snowmobile trail along an old road, hiking, cross-country skiing, snowshoeing

This route provides a good 3.5-mile walk to Dry and Dexter lakes and a better than 4 mile walk to Spectacle Lake. Because the trail follows an old logging road on level ground most of the way, it is not difficult to walk. Both Dry and Dexter are handsome little lakes with steep shores. Dexter can also be reached from the west, section 47, or by way of Spectacle Lake.

The snowmobile trail to Dry and Dexter lakes is most attractive in winter, when it makes an excellent ski route. If you continue on to Spectacle, either on skis or snowshoes, you can cross that lake's several lobes and return as described in section 71.

The marked trail begins opposite the parking turnout north of the second bridge on NY 10. The trail heads west for less than 0.5 mile to the intersection described in section 71, then continues straight ahead, taking a relatively level course on the lower, northern, slopes of Good Luck Mountain. The trail reaches Dry Lake after a gently-rolling course west for 2 miles from the intersection. The terrain is uniform at first, almost dull, but improves to become an agreeable woodland walk with vistas through the woods.

A gentle downhill and a southwest curve in the trail marks the approach to Dry Lake. The trail dips almost to shoreline at its northern corner, where there is a dry place for a picnic. The trail continues along the steep northwest shore, about 20 feet up on the hillside, perhaps 100 feet from the water's edge. If the ice is strong, it is easier to ski across to the southern tip, the outlet end. The trail continues to Dexter Lake from the southwestern end of Dry, 150 yards north of the outlet. It bears south of west through a draw for 0.5 mile, descending nearly 130 feet from Dry Lake.

The trail's approach to heart-shaped Dexter Lake is in a marshy, grassy area, where the trail is briefly overgrown. Continue along Dexter's southeast shore and quickly pick it up again. The trail continues along the shoreline for 0.3 mile to the outlet—there are actually two outlet streams flowing from a long, snaky beaver dam. Walk downstream a short distance to find a narrow enough crossing.

The remains of a large logging settlement lie in fields to the west of the outlet, where a continuing old road begins to head north along Dexter's west shore. The snowmobile route continues southwest, quickly reaching a junction with signs and mileages. The route east points toward Spectacle Lake, but the distance given is short. The mileage via this route to the Burnt Vly Trailhead is only off by 0.2 mile; the actual distance is 6.7 miles. The return distance is given as 4.1 miles, which is just a little longer than it really is. Mileage to Potter Homestead on the continuing southern route is given as 3 miles, when it really is 5 miles, section 47.

If you use this route to ski or snowshoe a 9-mile loop that includes Dry, Dexter, and Spectacle lakes, you can stop at the boulder island in Spectacle and explore that lake's islands and peninsulas. The descent into Dexter Lake can be steep for skis, but the rest of the trek is moderate.

Another winter alternative is suggested for snowshoers. Head toward Dry Lake, either following the trail or using the valley of State Brook for a part of that distance. Then head south across Dry Lake to its outlet end and follow the outlet to Spectacle. The 0.5-mile segment between the lakes is especially lovely with a little waterfall on the stream. There is no trail, but the outlet is easy to follow. You can head east to the far end of the eastern lobe and pick up the snowmobile trail back, or, if you are adept at bushwhacking in winter, try a route that involves a trek up part of Good Luck Mountain. From the outlet of Dry into Spectacle Lake, walk to the big rock in the lake, then head north up the western end of Good Luck Mountain. Along the top of the ridge there are rock outcrops with winter views toward the outlet of Canada Lake, 7 miles away. From the ridge, cross the mountain heading northeast and intersect the snowmobile trail again. The climb from Spectacle to the ridge is almost 500 feet, and the round-trip walk exceeds 8 miles. It is a very strenuous outing for which a minimum of six hours is required.

√ | 73 | Cliffs on Good Luck Mountain
Bushwhack

A path of sorts leads to these cliffs, but deadfalls and a couple of confusing points require that it be called a bushwhack. These cliffs are one of the most beautiful and unusual in the region and lie on the side of the eastern-most knob of Good Luck Mountain, which has a series of small summits. The cliffs cover a part of the southwest face of the eastern summit and are visible from Spectacle Lake. Beneath the cliff a tumble of huge boulders rises dramatically out of a long gorge.

As if the striking view of Spectacle Lake and Third and Fourth lakes were not enough, the panorama even includes, on a clear day, the hills that ring the Mohawk River to the south.

Take the snowmobile trail, section 71, toward Spectacle Lake. As you descend the hill and Good Luck Lake is visible to the east, you cross an intermittent stream on a six-foot bridge, climb a small rise, and descend to cross a second larger stream on a fifteen-to twenty-foot bridge. This is where you leave the trail. (Over the next rise is a much larger stream and marshy place with a forty-foot bridge. If you reach it, turn back.)

Turn off the trail on the near side of the second stream and follow it north and west, along a faint footpath. Just below the steep hill, the footpath crosses the stream that emerges from the draw below the cliffs. The path now climbs steeply on the west side of the stream, never more than 150 feet from the draw. The lower cliffs have great ice formations in winter. Needless to say, the hiking route described is a superb snowshoe trek in winter. It is a steep 600-foot climb to the summit.

Cliffs are visible almost from the beginning of the climb. If the footpath seems faint, stay close to the huge boulders that choke the valley beneath the cliffs. About two-thirds of the way to the top, you will reach the best outcrop. Here a huge rock slab shelters a small cave and the rock top gives views of the valley below and the cliffs above. That rock is in turn guarded by a giant rock spire that looms like the jaw of a prehistoric animal. There is so much to explore in the gorge!

Continue up the path 100 yards beyond the rocks. The path crosses the stream and heads steeply to a saddle below the cliffs. Continue through the saddle for 200 yards, beyond the cliffs, where the path turns right toward the mountain. Scramble up. The going is rough here and the way not clear—recent dead falls and a tangle of spruce obscure the route to the summit. At the height of land, you have to walk south and descend (no more than a 20-foot descent) into a small cleft in the summit and push

Good Luck Mountain Cliffs

through more spruce to the top of the cliffs.

A loop bushwhack is possible from the Dry and Dexter Lake snowmobile trail, from a point 350 yards west of the intersection, section 72. A course south-southwest to the summit of the east knob will take you to several outcrops with winter views. The first overlooks the West Branch Valley. The route then swings south around and below the summit to continue west along the southeast face of the summit past a second outcrop. Near the west side of the summit knob, the route dips into the small rift and climbs to the cliff top.

From NY 10 it is 1.2 miles to the stream along the trail, then 0.5 mile for the 600-foot bushwhack to the summit. If you bushwhack from the north, it is 0.7 mile to the turnoff point, and 0.6 mile from there to the summit. The round trip is a total of 3 miles, but it always takes much more than three hours, probably because there is so much to see.

74 Tomany Mountain
Abandoned trail, walking, snowshoeing

The view from the Tomany fire tower is shortened in almost all directions by mountains that rise nearly as high as Tomany, so it is not surprising that this tower is among the many that the state has closed. There is no view without the tower, so the closing is unfortunate, because there was a lovely vista of the many vlies in the very remote country to the southeast. In winter you can still enjoy views of the West Branch and surrounding mountains like Ely, State Brook, and Trout Lake from the snow banks that often pile high enough to allow views through the trees.

In spite of the closing of the tower, the trail to the summit is still open and relatively easy to follow. It is a good hour's walk to the top, a climb of 800 feet in just over 1 mile. The trail begins opposite the parking turnout on NY 10 that is 2.6 miles north of the second bridge over the Sacandaga. The trail rises steadily west of NY 10, crossing Shanty Brook and the Seeley snowmobile trail to Avery's. (The Seeley Trail generally parallels NY 10 from the four way intersection of section 71 to Avery's and on to Kennels Pond. Because its usefulness is limited to snowmobilers, it is not described in this guide, though intersections with it are noted.)

The Tomany Trail then veers to the southwest around the summit. The last 0.3 mile is a very steep climb up the southeast face.

✓ ## 75 Jockeybush Lake

Path, hiking, camping, fishing, snowshoeing

Several features distinguish Jockeybush Lake from other lakes in the high plateau bordered by the Powley-Piseco Road and NY 10. It is deep and cold, while most others are shallow and by midsummer quite warm. Many are the color of weak tea from dissolved tannins, but Jockeybush is unbelievably clear. The lake is 0.7 mile long but very narrow. It is bordered on the north and part of the south by steep, rocky hills covered by dense spruce and other evergreen thickets.

The path to Jockeybush Lake is pleasant and easy to walk; but because it is not well marked, it must be considered a path. The biggest problem with the markings is that the state has created a snowmobile trail parallel to NY 10 that connects the trails in the south near Good Luck Lake with the trails to the Powley-Piseco Road. The Jockeybush Lake route now shares a confusing trailhead with this connector.

The path begins from a parking turnout on the west side of NY 10, 0.3 mile north of Avery's Hotel and directly opposite the small man-made lake on the Avery property that boasts exotic water lilies. The way to Jockeybush is the northernmost of the two entrances.

It takes less than forty minutes to walk the 1.2-mile distance to the lake. For the first 0.2 mile, the path is north of Jockeybush Outlet, but after it crosses the stream, it generally follows it to the lake. You climb almost continuously, but gently, for the change in elevation between NY 10 and the lake is only 240 feet. In the last 200 yards below the natural dike outlet the path is a little obscured by a deep growth of ferns. Sometimes it seems to disappear altogether, but if you stay in the outlet valley, you will be on track.

Jockeybush is an ideal lake for a boat and sometimes a fishing boat is left at the outlet. If you have access to a boat, explore the far western end of the lake. There are a couple of small rock islands, and the view toward the outlet is especially lovely. The swimming is very good. The sloping rock on the north side of the outlet has been used for camping, though it is too close to water.

If you walk past the campsite on the north, you will find an informal path that leads west along the north shore. Sometimes high on the steep bank, sometimes close to shore, it leads to a small promontory about one-third of the way down the lake. If you are interested in a difficult bushwhack, this path will put you almost far enough down the shore so you can head north through the draw between the two hills toward Iron Lake, section 16.

76 Avery's Kennels Pond
Trails, cross-country skiing, fishing, snowmobiling

Kennels Pond is a private lake owned by the Avery family, who for most of this century have run the old frame hotel that overlooks the West Branch of the Sacandaga. You can fish, for a fee, and ski the network of trails around the pond. These have been cut through logged lands that make walking along the pond less than pleasant though their width makes them great for skiing. You need permission from the hotel or the caretaker at the pond to walk that trail, which connects with the Powley-Piseco Road, section 13.

History buffs will appreciate the note that Kennels Pond was named for Eli Kennell, originally Quesnell, a Canadian who owned 2200 acres between Avery's and the Shaker Place. He was the only man who would ride logs through the rapids below the Shaker Place dam on the West Branch. Those who venture into the wilderness to explore the wild gorge of the West Branch will be awed by this fact.

Several snowmobile trails converge at Avery's: a route that parallels NY 10 and leads to the "four corners" just north of Good Luck Lake, section 71, providing connection with numerous routes to the west and south; the trail from Clockmill Corners, section 13; and a route that roughly parallels NY 10 north to the Powley-Piseco Road. With the two northern trails and the Powley-Piseco Road, a giant circuit can be devised, providing 12.6 miles of excellent cross-country skiing. If you ski the loop from Kennels Pond, add 2 miles to reach the loop. If you ski the loop from the intersection of the Powley-Piseco Road and NY 10, add 2.4 miles to the loop. If parking is no problem, and it may be, you can start the loop at a point on NY 10, 1.6 miles south of its intersection with the Powley-Piseco Road. Here the snowmobile trail comes within fifty feet of the highway.

The 6-mile stretch from Teeter Creek Vly to NY 10 and on to the Powley-Piseco Road is level for the first 1.5 miles as it traverses marshes heading northeast. The trail then curves to the north and climbs 200 feet before descending sharply for an equal distance to its closest approach to NY 10. The trail then heads northwest, crosses spruce swamps and then climbs nearly 100 feet to the Powley-Piseco Road. Even with a good trail packed by snowmobiles, this is a strenuous route with many ups and downs and it entails a full day's skiing.

77 Confluence of Piseco Outlet and the West Branch

Bushwhack

This bushwhack route follows an old path that sportsmen would dub a "clear trail." Once the beginning is found, the foottread is obvious in summer; but lack of marking makes it all but impossible to follow on snowshoes in winter.

The path provides a chance to walk to the confluence of these two streams for fishing or for picnicking. Among the many paths that Adirondack fishermen have carved out of the wilderness to their favorite spots, few are as lovely as that to the confluence of the Piseco Outlet and the West Branch of the Sacandaga. This place is tantalizing because there is no trail along the river beyond this junction until it emerges from the trackless wilderness, 3 miles to the northeast, where paths from Whitehouse and elsewhere to the east dwindle away.

The path to the confluence starts opposite the northern third of the parking turnout on west side of NY 10; the turnout is 1.7 miles north of the road to Shaker Place and 2.7 miles south of the bridge over Big Bay of Piseco Lake. The path forks right as it leaves roadside and can be difficult to spot.

The path leads generally east for 0.7 mile, traversing open woods that are dark and damp enough to support a lush growth of varied mosses. These occur in the last third of the way in wet areas where the footpath is narrow, overgrown, and not always obvious, requiring the designation of this route as a bushwhack.

The last two hundred feet take you through a swampy meadow with alders, which means that finding the route for the return will be especially difficult. The path then turns to cross a small, wooden footbridge over the North Vly Stream. That stream flows in from the west and the bridge is less than 300 feet from where it joins Piseco Outlet in an open marsh.

You emerge from a spruce thicket on the shore of the outlet beside a lovely stillwater set off by small rapids to the north and south. Head downstream; it is easy walking on the bank above the outlet. As the stream flows over rapids on its way south, a small island breaks it into two channels.

The West Branch flows in from the south 0.7 mile along the outlet. Both streams are quiet and deep at the confluence, and the banks are covered with alders so that there are but one or two spots where it is easy to walk to the water's edge. The path really seems to end here, and there is no obvious point where either stream can be forded, even in low water, without hip waders. Both streams have deep and lovely pools close to where they merge.

This route unquestionably makes a choice short walk. No more than two hours are required to complete the trip, and there are several spots where picnickers could enjoy the tranquil eddies on Piseco Outlet.

78 West Branch below Shaker Place
Canoeing

For those who enjoy exploring the West Branch by water, the path to the confluence of it and Piseco Outlet, section 77, offers the only portage route to the quiet stretch between Shaker Place and the gorge area. The 1.2-mile carry is possible with a light canoe. Launch your canoe in the still-water below the islands in Piseco Outlet almost 0.5 mile downstream from the path's first approach to the outlet near the North Vly crossing. The last 0.3 mile of Piseco Outlet is navigable, and from the confluence you can either paddle the West Branch 1.5 miles upstream before reaching rapids or 0.8 mile downstream before coming on the first rapids and set of waterfalls in the gorge area, section 101.

There are many advantages to portaging a canoe to this part of the stream. It provides access to a marvelous trek through West Branch country and makes it easy to reach a beautiful campsite at the uppermost set of falls. There are trout in the West Branch, but the best fishing is nearby on Moose Creek, and a canoe is almost the only way to reach that stream. It flows north into the West Branch 0.8 mile upstream from the confluence.

The longish portage may at first deter you from bringing a canoe to this point by way of this route, but do not be tempted to paddle downstream from Shaker Place instead. There are rapids just below Shaker Place, and even though it is a simple matter to carry around them to the flowed lands downstream, that canoeable stretch lasts for only 1 mile. Beyond, a long series of rapids stretches 0.8 mile downstream. In high water this portion of stream would be a difficult whitewater run, and in low water, the river has more rocks than water. Portaging and lining the 0.8-mile stretch of rapids is very difficult.

South of Piseco Lake

THE AREA AROUND Piseco Lake is an excellent place to look for accommodations within easy driving distance of most of the paths, picnic spots, and other delights in this guidebook. Three state campgrounds, Point Comfort, Little Sand Point, and Poplar Point, are located on the northwest shore of Piseco, nestled beneath the handsome mountains that rim the lake. In addition, many guest houses and motels can be found in the area bounded by Piseco, Oxbow Lake, and Lake Pleasant. A fourth campground, Moffit Beach, is at Sacandaga Lake near Speculator.

Except for the campgrounds, most of the accessible lake shores and most of the land adjacent to NY 8 in the vicinity of Piseco Lake is private. Further, the best trail on the south side of NY 8, the one to Hamilton Mountain, is no longer available. Even if you could reach the summit of Hamilton Mountain, with its tower now removed there is no longer any view. Only one other place, the cliffs on Finch Mountain, afford a glimpse of the secret interior of the West Branch Valley, and those cliffs can be reached only by bushwhacking, section 97.

79 Big Bay of Piseco and Piseco Outlet
Canoeing, fishing

If the wind is calm and you are looking for a good open-water canoe trip, you may wish to explore the shores and corners of the 2.5-mile-long Big Bay at the outlet of Piseco. You can put a canoe in at the Piseco Lake outlet on NY 8 or at the western end of the bay where it is bridged by NY 10.

Big Bay is certainly not remote, and because of motor boats, it would be best to canoe here in the spring or fall when there are generally fewer people around. The Bay is so wide, up to 0.25 mile in places, that the views of the surrounding country are not as limited as those on trips through more marshy and narrower streams. Irondequoit and Panther Mountains loom to the north, a scenic backdrop to the heavily wooded shores. However, the width and length of open water also mean that it can become very rough in windy weather. So, while water level has no effect on this trip, wind must definitely be considered. The entire jagged shoreline can be explored in three hours, and if it were not for other boat traffic and the proximity to civilization, a canoe trip on Big Bay would be considered choice.

Along the Northville-Placid Trail south of Piseco

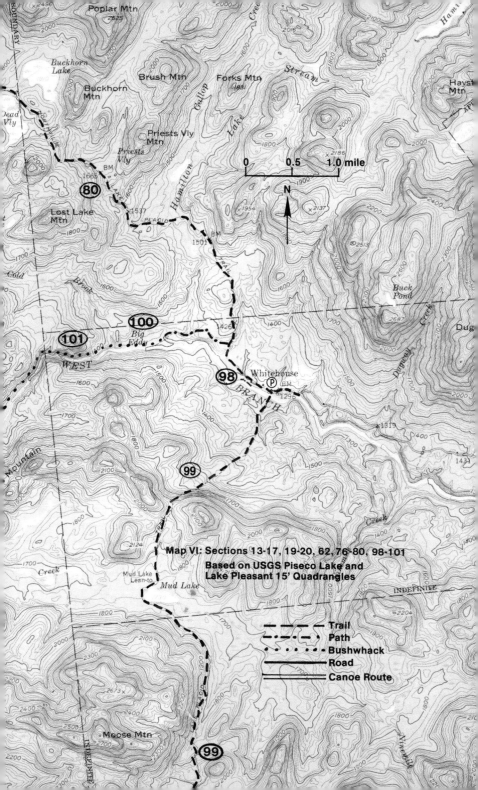

Map VI: Sections 13-17, 19-20, 62,76-80, 98-101
Based on USGS Piseco Lake and
Lake Pleasant 15' Quadrangles

Trail
Path
Bushwhack
Road
Canoe Route

A very pleasant day's adventure can be made out of the canoe trip east from NY 10 through part of Piseco Outlet. There is a dam across the outlet just east of NY 10, and there are a few rapids downstream of it, but the rest of the route is a leisurely excursion through marshy grasslands and swampy meanders where there is little current.

Although an experienced white water canoer might want to launch just below the dam, it is easiest to portage on the snowmobile trail east off NY 10 on the north side of the bridge. From here Piseco Outlet is broad and bordered with pickerel-weed as it flows in a generally eastward direction.

After almost 1 mile, the stream turns sharply north in a big bend and before turning south a small stream comes in from the north. This is the outlet of Spy Lake, and it is possible, if beaver have been active, to canoe up into Spy Lake. Don't be deterred by the fact that the stream is narrow and winds about a great deal through the swamp. A few small beaver dams also necessitate brief canoe carries, but they keep the water high enough so that you do not have to drag your canoe through the shallow parts.

This side trip provides quite a bit of excitement. There are many signs of beaver and the 300 yards immediately downstream of Spy Lake have a beautiful, arched tree cover of swamp maple. Watch for bitterns along the shore. The excursion into Spy Lake is 1 mile long, and you can explore the lake. The view from the outlet across the lake is of Echo Cliffs on Panther Mountain.

Beyond Spy Lake Outlet, Piseco Outlet flows south for another 0.5 mile along a level course. Part way south along the east side, the outlet of another Mud Lake flows in from the east; the view to the east here is of Mud Lake Mountain. It is possible to canoe up the outlet and through Mud Lake, carrying over a beaver dam and passing several very large but quite old beaver houses on the way. Mud Lake has a swampy border, part of which is a real quaking sphagnum bog complete with rose pogonia blooming in mid-July, cranberries in fall, as well as other typical bog plants. See the description of Chub Lake, section 65, for what to expect.

80   Northville-Placid Trail from Piseco to Whitehouse

Hiking, camping, snowshoeing, cross-country skiing
6.7 miles, 3½ hours, 500-foot descent

This section of the Northville-Placid Trail is the only route through the wilderness immediately south and east of NY 8 and 10. If you can arrange to have a car at both ends, the trail makes a good one-day outing as a trip into the heart of West Branch country; though a day hike from either end can be pleasant. The middle of the trail is by far the most interesting.

There are excellent camping opportunities along the route. The west end of the trail is adjacent to the Piseco School on NY 8, opposite the intersection of Old Piseco Road, and 3.4 miles northeast of the intersection of NY 8 and 10. The trailhead is marked, and the trail enters an open field and heads diagonally across it to the south. Markings are scarce and the way is not obvious but you will pick up markers clearly at the south end of the field.

While it is traditional to walk the Northville-Placid Trail from south to north, you will probably find it more pleasant to walk this segment from north to south, moving from civilization into remote country. This is the easiest way, for you will be walking generally downhill rather than up. The Whitehouse trailhead is described on page 137.

The trail takes a fairly level course for the first 1.4 miles to the outlet of Buckhorn Lake along a long abandoned roadway. The high (1810-foot) mountain lake lies to the north of the trail. The guideboard at the trailhead calls this Fiddlers Lake and gives the distance as 1.8 miles. A short bushwhack leads along the outlet to marshes surrounding its southern end.

Continuing southeast, the trail crosses the shoulder of a small hill, and descends 200 feet in an easterly direction. At 2.6 miles you approach Priest's Vly and turn south along the vly to cross its outlet at 2.8 miles. You hop rocks below the beaver dam, which at present holds little water in the vly. (If you are walking south to north, cross the outlet and walk in the tall grasses beside the vly for 50 feet to pick up the continuing faint trail.)

The next mile or so are the loveliest on the whole route. You wander over a small rise, then descend steeply to cross a tributary of Hamilton Lake Stream at 3.5 miles, again hopping rocks. The trail parallels the stream then rises briefly. At 3.7 miles, a left, north, fork leads 50 yards to a lean-to overlooking that stream. You find a stretch of boardwalk of half-log stringers, a small bridge, and a drying beaver marsh in the next 0.3 mile, all this while walking through a nice spruce and hemlock stand. At 4 miles the huge suspension bridge looms over a deep, quiet stretch of Hamilton Lake Stream.

East of the bridge, the trail becomes wider—the ruts from the old wagon road are obvious. The trail curves southeast and is relatively level; the forest cover is notable for a few huge maples, with stands of Christmas fern beneath. Even though some of the trees are quite magnificent, the 1.8-mile stretch to an intersection is a bit dull. Just before 5.8 miles you climb briefly to intersect the road west, section 98. Your route straight ahead is a veritable highway of a trail, leading at 6.5 miles to the sign-in register.

The way south leads to the West Branch, and straight at 6.7 miles to the parking area for Whitehouse.

A round trip walk to Priest's Vly from Piseco takes three hours; a round trip walk to the vly from the south and Whitehouse takes three and a half to four hours. If you are out for a stroll, especially in fall when most of the leaves have fallen, there is a bushwhack near the Piseco Trailhead that offers views of Buckhorn Pond. Rogers Mountain is one of the series of conical mountains that line NY 8. To reach vantages on it, walk south on the Northville Placid Trail for five minutes to a height of land and pick a course of due north. You traverse level ground and one slightly wet area for nearly ten minutes before beginning to climb this steep 700-foot tall mountain through a forest of tall maples. Continue north, staying fairly close to the western flanks. The route is like a giant staircase, open rock slabs alternating with steep pitches. At about the 2280-foot level (an altimeter really helps here) you should find an open rock patch with year-round views across Piseco Lake to Panther, Piseco, and Stacey mountains, with T Lake and Twin Mountains on the horizon behind. The view south is over Little Lake to the marshes around Piseco Outlet. Continue climbing slightly and working to the east around Rogers Mountain to find grassy patches in an open oak forest. These are still nearly 200 feet short of the summit and they offer fall or spring views over Buckhorn Pond to the heart of the Silver Lake Wilderness. A compass bearing west of south brings you back to the Northville-Placid Trail. This bushwhack takes no more than two hours from the trail.

Benson Road

BENSON ROAD CONNECTS Caroga Lake and NY 10 on the west with NY 30 on the east, 3 miles north of Northville. The eastern two-thirds of the road generally follows West Stony Creek as it flows northeast toward the Sacandaga River. Although the road gives access to Shaker Mountain Wild Forest and Silver Lake Wilderness, much of the land along it is private. Among the few exceptions in the nearly twenty-mile-long, sparsely-settled road are Pinnacle Road, the Northville-Placid Trailhead in Upper Benson, Cathead Mountain, Woods Lake, and two access routes to West Stony Creek. The private land on both sides of the road has been and continues to be logged.

Trails at the west end of Benson Road have been covered in the chapter on Canada Lake. If you are driving east on Benson Road, you will find views at 8.3 miles to the mountains north of Northville. At the Bleeker-Benson town line, a little under 10 miles from Caroga, you see first Wallace Mountain, then as the road turns you see Three Ponds Mountain to the west and Cathead to the east. It is a rare trip in summer when ruffed grouse or pheasants with young are not spotted beside the road. Infrequent traffic and sparse settlement make this paved highway appear desolate.

81 Pinnacle Road
Hiking, camping, snowshoeing

Pinnacle Road, marked only with a sign for Chase Lake, heads north-northwest from Benson Road, 6.6 miles east of NY 10, 11.7 miles west of NY 30. The road crosses Holmes Lake Outlet at 0.5 mile—marshes to the west fill what was once a dammed pond called Peters Pond. It served as power for the Peter's sawmills from the 1880s until about 1915.

Marshes lie to the east of a second bridge, this one over Pinnacle Creek, at 1.3 miles. Both places invite the birder to stop. At 1.4 miles, there is a snowmobile trail to the west, leading to the trail to Holmes Lake, section 27. A beaver marsh floods that trail in 0.4 mile, but do stop and walk along the first part of the trail. The old road it follows has firm, soft footing; the route traverses a lovely hemlock forest; and the beaver pond at 0.4 mile has birds and butterflies.

Return to your car and continue north over another bridge on Pinnacle Creek at 1.6 miles. At 2.6 miles you pass the last house on the road and just beyond reach a small parking turnout and the trailhead for Chase Lake.

Pinnacle Road, now only a path, continues north-northwest for 2.4 miles to the height-of-land in a draw between Panther and Pigeon Mountains. Walking here can be more pleasant than along the Chase Lake Trail. Wildlife abounds, deer, rabbits, owls, and numerous birds and ducks. The forests and marshes are exceptionally handsome; you will spot the giant pad-leaf orchid in June.

The old roadway heads steeply up a ridge of Pinnacle Mountain and joins and follows Pinnacle Creek after 0.2 mile. The road climbs beneath Pinnacle Mountain, following the stream through a deep hemlock forest. The grade eases, but the road continues to climb through the steep gorge.

Notice the heavy planking in the roadway, hemlock posts that have survived for decades. Notice also the wonderful old wooden culverts that keep most of the roadway dry. After half an hour of walking, the roadway becomes more level; you cross a tributary of Pinnacle Creek at 1.2 miles on a tiny bridge constructed of old timbers; there are marshes off to the left.

Beyond, the roadway climbs again. Watch closely now, for there are foundations on both sides of the road and rockwork in the stream. This is the site of the Pinnacle sawmill. The foundations continue for several hundred feet. The roadway traverses a grassy meadow, part of the old settlement at 1.4 miles; there is a cellar hole to the right of the field. A dam once flooded the marshy area that fills the upland valley that follows. The roadway, sheltered with tall trees, continues beside the marsh. Tall maples and yellow birch mix with evergreens. There are glimpses of Pigeon Mountain and the high plateau to the west. A large beaver house dominates a newly flooded place in the stream.

The roadway, now narrower, continues beside the stream, climbing the deep valley between Pigeon and Panther Mountains. You pass the site of a fall hunting camp at 2.2 miles, and the road seems to end. However, paths lead left and right through the two draws to the north. The right, east, path follows a roadway for 0.2 mile to a saddle and continues downhill. Bushwhackers note that the way left provides a convenient beginning for a bushwhack west up the plateau of Pigeon Mountain to the cluster of lakes to the west of it—County Line, Little Oxbarn, Fisher Vly, Winter, and Duck.

While it takes little more than an hour for the 600-foot climb, you can easily spend half a day or more birding, exploring, and just enjoying.

Along Pinnacle Road

82 Chase Lake

Hiking, fishing, camping, birding, cross-country skiing
2.6 miles, 1¼ hours, relatively level

The route from the end of Pinnacle Road, section 81, to Chase Lake is an officially designated and marked snowmobile trail that follows old logging roads. It also has some yellow hiking trail markers. The trail describes a circuitous route to avoid private land and joins the traditional trail, which left Pinnacle Road in the vicinity of the Beagle and Hare Club. There are many old logging roads in the vicinity as well as a shorter road that once served as the principal route to Chase Lake. The trail swings up the Pinnacle Valley and then connects with a road that swings back southeast, meeting the road from the Beagle Club access where it heads east to the lake. The trails and intersections are adequately marked, though sometimes these markings have been reported missing. Take a compass and map to make sure you choose the proper directions.

The trail passes through high open woods, sometimes hardwoods, sometimes stands of evergreens, with many spring wildflowers and good birding near the lake.

The trail begins in a very wet area; circle around it to the left. The first 200 yards of trail has been cut to avoid private land and within five minutes you meet and turn left, northeast, on a nice old woods road. Continue northeast for 0.4 mile, then east, angling left into the woods on a narrower trail. As the trail angles southeast, making the detour around private land, you descend two short little hills—the only real ones in the entire route. The second gives skiers pause. Beyond the bridge over the stream in the second draw, the trail climbs almost due south. A route marked with red rectangles joins from the right and these markings continue along your trail for 0.2 mile. You are at the edge of land that has been logged.

At 1 mile, nearly half an hour walk, the trail intersects a woods road. Turn left, northeast. The woods to this point have been good, but what follows is really lovely. The trail (old road) follows a draw that is to your right. It is filled with hemlock. You cross two small streams draining toward the draw, one with a decrepit bridge of old logs, the other with a fairly decent bridge. You follow the draw for about 0.8 mile, twenty minutes, and descend to cross the small stream that creates the draw. Beyond, your route is generally east and almost level for another 0.8 mile, until the small descent west of the lake.

The trail reaches Chase Lake on a fairly dry promontory between two large marshy areas. There is a lean-to, and often a fair amount of trash

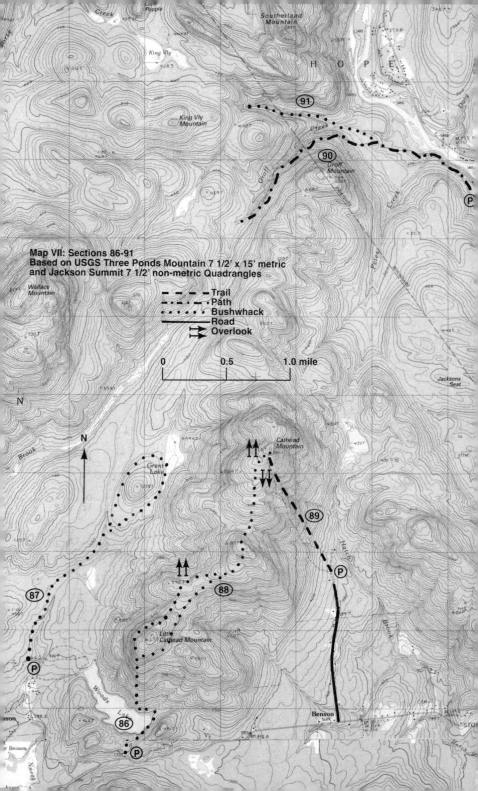

Map VII: Sections 86-91
Based on USGS Three Ponds Mountain 7 1/2' x 15' metric
and Jackson Summit 7 1/2' non-metric Quadrangles

- - - Trail
-·-·- Path
······· Bushwhack
——— Road
⇉ Overlook

0   0.5   1.0 mile

N

N

and garbage. Sometimes there is a boat. You cannot easily walk around the lake, so either a boat or skis in winter are needed to see much of it.

83 Silver Lake via the Northville-Placid Trail

Hiking, camping, cross-country skiing
7.5 miles, 3½ hours, 770-foot vertical rise

Silver Lake lies in the middle of West Branch country and its outlet is a major source of the West Branch of the Sacandaga. Trails to the lake start either from the Benson Road or Whitehouse, section 97.

Traditionally, the Northville-Placid Trail follows the Benson Road from NY 30 to Upper Benson, a distance of 6.0 miles. It is unfortunate that this part of the trail follows a road, not a woodsy trail. There has been talk for years of rerouting this section, but no action has been taken. However, the open route does permit views of distant mountains, which are not visible along much of the rest of the trail. At Benson, at 6.0 and 6.1 miles, the trail makes two right turns, leading back east along Washburn Road for 0.5 mile, where it turns northwest on Godfrey Road. At this intersection, a sign gives the distance to Silver Lake as 7.5 miles. The most accessible trailhead is 0.5 mile farther down Godfrey Road, at a designated place and sign-in booth.

If you are traveling from the west along Benson Road to the Northville-Placid Trailhead, you will come to a sign for it 10.5 miles from NY 10. Where the Benson Road curves right, the trail is straight ahead on Washburn Road.

The round-trip walk is just short of 15 miles, making it a long one-day trek. The traditional trailhead, which can now be reached only by four-wheel-drive vehicles, is another 1.3 miles northwest on the extension of Godfrey Road. From there, the 12.4-mile round trip is still a pretty stiff one-day hike.

From the designated trailhead, the route, sparsely marked with blue disks, is along a road that passes quickly through private land and then continues northwest up a gentle rise and around the base of a low hill to the old parking lot by the North Branch of West Stony Creek. From here the trail heads southwest 0.3 mile to cross the creek on a new hiker's bridge and continue west into the wilderness. Compared with other West Branch routes, this seems like a superhighway, groomed too perfectly and traveled too much.

At 2.5 miles, 0.9 mile past Stony Creek, the trail crosses Goldmine Creek, again without benefit of bridge. An 1886 clipping from the Fulton County

North Branch, West Stony Creek, near Northville-Placid Trail

Republican refers to a fire that "destroyed the goldmine works." These works were vaguely located in the southern part of Hamilton County. Was the mine near Goldmine Creek; was gold ever really found near here; or was this one of the numerous salted mines?

The trail heads northwest, then continues generally west following a fairly level course to a junction 4.6 miles. A short spur to the left leads to a campsite on Rock Lake.

The trail crosses the West Branch of the Sacandaga, here a small stream, at 5.7 miles, and makes a sharp turn to the north. The relatively level east-west portion of the trail so far has made this a favorite for wilderness cross-country skiing, and the trail's breadth makes it perfectly suited for this use. Out of sight at the stream crossing to the south are marshes surrounding the stream. Skiers enjoy leaving the trail and bushwhacking south to explore those marshes.

Beyond the stream crossing, the trail north continues for a time beside the stream through a narrow draw. The trail climbs 250 feet in the next 0.9 mile to Meco Lake; it is the steep grade on the return that makes continuing on this trail difficult for skiers.

After passing Meco Lake, which lies to the east of the trail at 6.5 miles, you descend slightly to Silver Lake and round the eastern end to the lean-to at 7.5 miles.

Silver Lake is most often a camping destination. The lakeshores are a bit muddy for swimming. Its deep clear waters used to be among the best for fishing, but the pH has been too low for trout to reproduce for nearly a decade. Coyotes serenade the lean-to in the evening with a mournful and piercing cry.

Note that because of the steep section south of Meco Lake, the trip to Silver Lake is recommended only for experienced skiers and only those adept at long wilderness treks should try the round trip.

84 Benson Tract Bushwhacks

While almost all of the 50,000 acres of Benson Tract was logged before the 1880s, only the large spruce, those 19" and over at the butt end, were taken in a cut that barely disturbed the woods. Most of the tract was acquired by the State for lapsed taxes, a few lots were purchased outright, and a half dozen of the 160-acre lots were resold in the early 1890s, logged, and reacquired by the State in 1900. The resale was possible because the

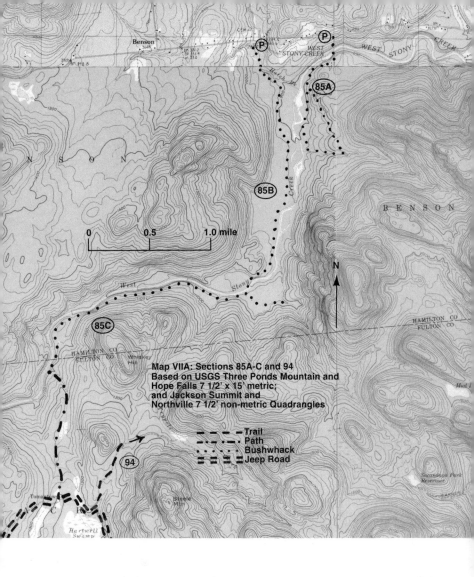

Map VIIA: Sections 85A-C and 94
Based on USGS Three Ponds Mountain and
Hope Falls 7 1/2' x 15' metric;
and Jackson Summit and
Northville 7 1/2' non-metric Quadrangles

— — — Trail
— · — Path
· · · · · Bushwhack
▪ ▪ ▪ Jeep Road

forest had recovered so thoroughly from the earlier logging that a second cut was possible. The logging roads from this second cut, which branch out from the old Northville-Placid Trailhead clearing at the North Branch of West Stony Creek, served as hunters' paths for years and some of them are still quite easy to follow. An exception is the road that led up Three Ponds Mountain. That route has all but disappeared, so the nine-hour trek that climbs 1300 feet up the mountain to the ponds and on to Helldevil Dam and return is now an extremely difficult bushwhack, so difficult that this guide will give general rather than specific route indications.

To begin any of the bushwhacks, you have to ford Stony Creek, so you will not want to do them in high water. To ford the creek, head a bit to the right through the clearing where the Northville-Placid Trail makes a left turn to the west. On the north side, you can easily find the logging road. In 200 yards the road crosses two small streambeds, usually dry washes, and enters a small field.

84A Abner Creek Bushwhack

Twenty feet into the field a road forks right, crosses the stream that flows from the Notch and continues northeast. After the initial climb up from the streambed, the route is relatively level. After a little more than a 0.5 mile, you see the marshes that surround Abner Creek off to your right. The roadway continues on the slopes above the marshes, still heading northeast, but now following Abner Creek. After skirting the marshes for a little more than 0.5 mile, the roadway draws close to the valley floor. Remarkable second growth hemlock stands dot sections of the broad valley. The roadway, rising again above the valley floor, continues to be visible all the way to the site of an old sawmill. You can follow the valley northeast past beaver marshes to the height-of-land, from the north side of which flows Groff Creek, section 90. The through trip, for those who have scouted and understand the terrain, is still a challenging bushwhack.

84B The Notch

Easier to follow than the old road to Abner Creek is the roadway north from the field, that is its easy once you have found the place it leaves the field described above. Start through the field, walking fifty feet past the right fork to Abner Creek, and turn left. In a few feet you intersect the road, whose beginning is usually concealed by tall field plants. This roadway is a gem. It follows the stream from the Notch but high above it for two-thirds of a mile to a fork. The left fork continues two hundred yards to a stream crossing and some old foundations. The right fork continues just over that distance, but downhill, to cross the outlet of two of the Three Ponds.

The right fork, heading a little east of north, is very lovely. For a third of a mile it stays close to the Notch Brook, then crosses the brook and climbs high on the east side of the very narrow valley. There are lovely camping sites along the route and more as the roadway enters the Notch between Three Ponds and Wallace mountains, where the roadway disappears.

84C Three Ponds Mountain and Helldevil Dam

Unfortunately the left fork in the old road, which could be followed up the slopes of Three Ponds Mountain two decades ago, is mostly overgrown and not worth searching for. From the stream crossing, the easiest route is northwest up the gentlest slopes of the mountain, staying to the west of the outlet of the ponds. You will want to draw closer to the outlet as you approach the level of the ponds—an altimeter is helpful for this trek. No matter how you approach the ponds, the top of the mountain is dense spruce.

If you find the ponds without too much effort, continue to the third, the northern one, and follow its outlet west and then northwest to Helldevil Dam, the site of a flood dam for the earliest logging operations in Benson Tract, dating to 1870 or before. The northern of the Three Ponds and Helldevil Dam are the headwaters of Ninemile Creek, which flows north into the West Branch of the Sacandaga. To return by a different route from Helldevil Dam, follow its other inlet southeast past the marsh that is sometimes the fourth pond on the mountain. Keep the same direction through a pass and pick up a small stream. Stay to the east and uphill from that stream. This route will lead you back to the Notch roads.

85 West Stony Creek Approaches
Bushwhacks

The valley surrounding the lower reaches of West Stony Creek and the borders of Benson Road were logged and farmed many years ago. Much of Benson Road is privately owned, limiting access to West Stony Creek. Paths and bushwhacks, often using the route of old roads, provide three ways to explore the creek.

85A The Bridge and the Cemetery

The easiest approach to the lands south of West Stony Creek requires low water. A very narrow piece of state land, barely more than the width of the abandoned roadway, forks south from Benson Road 1.45 miles west of NY 30. Spotting the roadway is the hard part, though the stone walls that border it should be a clue if the Forest Preserve sign should be missing. The old road leads gently downhill for a quarter mile to the ruins of an old bridge. Rock-hopping just upstream is usually a wet affair, so bring sneaks for the crossing. On the south side, the continuing roadway heads west along the creek. Near an island, the creek bends south and the roadway does likewise until it reaches a fork. The right fork is not an old roadway, but it is well enough defined to be the route by which you will return.

The more obvious route is left, uphill, about 0.5 mile to a flat area in a Scotch pine plantation that fills a former farmstead. Below the flat area to the right you can find a small, old cemetery, but you will surely have to search about for it. The roadway ends, but continue through the flat area to the draw on the far side. Follow this draw with its tiny stream downhill and west toward West Stony Creek—this is a lovely stretch.

When you reach the bluff above West Stony Creek, turn right. Stay on the bench above the creek where you should pick up a path that leads to the earlier fork. Follow it back to the intersection. The whole is no more than a three hour walk.

85B Hatch Brook

The most rewarding approach to West Stony Creek is via Hatch Brook. The beginning is State land and a small detour will take you around the only private land you will meet on a trek south to a big bend in the creek. On the way you will pass through wonderful second growth stands of hemlock, you will look out on the islands that fill the creek, and in low water, you can ford the creek to reach an access to the cliffs on the unnamed hill that borders the creek on the east.

In the hollow of the Benson Road, 2.1 miles east of NY 30, park on the south side of the road. Head south into the woods, across a small tributary of Hatch Brook and immediately find a path along an old road through a reforestation area. The route takes you close to Hatch Brook on a bench above the brook. Within ten minutes, the brook bends to the east and you should spot yellow blazes. If you continued straight you would enter a mucky area on private land. Instead, turn right along the property line, which is heading south. A sort-of-path follows the line. Across the second of two small streams, the line approaches the hillside, which is on your right. Angle left here across the southern border of the line for a hundred yards to the bench which is high above the wetlands and marshes. Note this spot well for your return.

Follow the bench, still heading south, a direction that will take you through the hemlock stand. Twice the bench is cut by small streams flowing from the hill to the west. Beyond the second cut you will be attracted east to West Stony Creek, having avoided all the wetlands and marshes. A path continues on the bench above the creek all the way to the big bend. You pass several nice campsites, look out at the islands, and enjoy the lovely forest all along the route. The upstream end of the second island is the shallowest crossing if that is your goal. If seeking quiet along the creek is what you want, allow at least three hours for the trek to the bend and return.

85C Tomantown

From Tomantown, just west of Hartnell Swamp, see section 94, a logging road, on private land, heads north. Walking the mile-long road is best, but that makes the suggested trek a very long one. In the northernmost quarter mile, the roadway descends to Stony Creek. From here you can follow the creek, walking along its shores in low water, walking back in the lovely woods where the going is usually quite easy. Public land stretches from just east of the roadway all the way to (and beyond) the big northern bend in the creek.

You will want to walk at least as far east as the confluence of Trypoli Creek, for here the forest is of impressive hemlocks. The forest gets even better just beyond in the raised flat area to the south of the bend, through which flows the outlet of Mud Lake, section 95. From several points along the creek you can look east and up to the tantalizing cliffs in the northern range of the Benson hills.

86 Woods Lake

Short path, walking, picnicking, camping, fishing, canoeing

Because the walk to Woods Lake is so short and its wooded southern shore is so lovely, this route attracts numerous people. Do not go on weekends, but wait for a mid-week day. The path is on the north side of Benson Road, 4.6 miles west of NY 30. It begins opposite a small parking turnout on the south side of a sharp bend in the road. There are no markings to indicate the lake or the path.

The path is only 0.2 mile long through open woods formed by tall hemlocks whose needles make a soft, cushioned path and carpet the shores of the lake. Because of much use and the lake's proximity to the road, the camping area at the southeast corner is not always clean. There are private lands at the northern end of the lake, but the rest of the shoreline is owned by the state.

Several campsites dot the long southwestern shore, connected by informal paths. The farthest are free of road noises, which sometimes reach the southern corner of the lake.

The view up the lake is spectacular, dominated by Three Ponds Mountain in the distance with Little Cathead rising steeply from the lake's northeastern shore. Because the lake has such beautiful clear water, this is a lovely place to explore by canoe. The carry is short and easy. With a canoe you have the easiest access to the cliffs on the west face of Little Cathead, section 88.

87 Lapland Lake

Trails, cross-country skiing

Lapland Lake is a commercial cross-country ski center on a large tract of land that borders the northwest corner of Woods Lake. Signs on the Benson Road indicate a turn north to Lapland Lake Center 5 miles west of NY 30 and 0.8 mile east of Washburn Road and the signs for the Northville-Placid Trail. The ski center is less than a mile north of Benson Road.

A day-use fee is charged for cross-country skiers. Accomodations are available, contact Lapland Lake Nordic Ski and Vacation Center, RD2, Northville, NY 12134; telephone 518-863-4974.

Eighteen miles of trails are available. A novice loop using over 3 miles of woods roads connects the center to the lake where there are lovely views of the frozen expanse and the cliffs on Little Cathead, which seem suspended above. An intermediate loop winds within the novice loop, cutting through a spruce forest and crossing several small streams on handsome wooden bridges. An advanced loop, south of the novice loop, traverses a hemlock forest. There are lovely views from it into the deep woods.

Several advanced loops also range across the hillside west of the ski lodge. Maps for the trails are available at the lodge. The lower parts of the trails are in a deep pine reforestation area, but the upper slopes reach hardwood forests. The trails have been well designed and some have been widened to accommodate both traditional skiers and those using the skating technique.

A trail to Grant Lake is accessible from the trails of Lapland Lake. The trek, mostly over State-owned lands, offers a wilderness ski-touring experience for which you will need a map and you should tell them of your plans when you register at the ski center. The route, variously marked with red disks, loops past the north end of Grant Lake, then winds south, rejoining the route out just north of a lovely beaver marsh.

88 Little Cathead Mountain
Easy bushwhack, snowshoeing

This is another of my favorite bushwhacks that is most pleasant as a snowshoe trek. The southwestern face of Little Cathead, rising steeply from Woods Lake, is ringed with cliffs, a few with good summer views and many with fine winter views. The approach is via the Woods Lake path from Benson Road, section 86. Walk north along the southeastern shore, skirt the marsh in the northeast corner of the lake, and then follow the northern shore west for less than 0.3 mile. In summer, if you have a canoe, you can shorten the trek around the lake; and, of course, in winter you can snowshoe directly north from the path toward the mountain.

The cliffs lie below the summit and west of it. A bushwhack route almost due north along the long sloping ridge touching the lake's north shore will take you to them. The best vantage is below the uppermost cliffs, but that point cannot be safely reached in winter. You will probably spot several open places with views, some looking directly across Woods Lake and some looking south to the mountains beyond Benson Road.

The climb is a little over 0.5 mile long from the north shore of the lake, making the total one-way distance from the road just over 1 mile. The cliffs are about 600 feet above the lake, and in winter you need only an hour and a half to reach them.

A more difficult variation will take you northeast from the first vantage along the top of the range of cliffs to a spot with a commanding view south.

Continue northeast across the mountain but below the summit to an opening with a view to the north and Cathead Mountain. You can neither walk nor snowshoe down the cliff areas to the west, but if you walk far enough to the north you can descend through a steep draw. After dropping down more than 400 feet and heading west through the draw, turn to the south to circle back at the foot of the cliffs. You may even want to climb a small shoulder from the bottom of the draw to hug the bottom of the cliffs as closely as possible. That way you will have the best view of the ice formations on the cliffs. In winter the walk at the base of the cliffs is dramatic.

When you are ready to leave, circle around to the southeast below the cliffs through a valley and return to the shore of the lake. The entire circuit, from Benson Road, requires about four hours of walking time and covers a total of 3.5 miles.

89 Cathead Mountain

Hiking, snowshoeing
1.25 miles, 1¼ hours, 1100-foot vertical rise

A good trail leads to the manned fire tower on Cathead Mountain, where there is a most impressive view. Mountains on the west and north block distant views into the interior of West Branch country, but the swampy lands surrounding Grant Lake on the west and the vista from there to Three Ponds Mountain give a good impression of how rugged and heavily wooded the region is. The panorama to the east across Great Sacandaga Lake is spectacular. Best of all, on a clear day it is possible to pick out a few of the High Peaks on the horizon in the north and see as far as the Capital District on the southeast.

A sign at North Road, 2.8 miles west of NY 30 on Benson Road marks the turn north to the trailhead for the fire tower. Drive north for 1.2 miles and park, being careful not to block either the continuing logging road or the driveway for the private home at the end of the road.

The trail, which heads toward magnetic north for the steep climb, begins on a dirt road that is barred to vehicular traffic. After 100 yards the trail branches left from the dirt road. Take the left turn and notice the row of telephone lines. The trail runs beneath the telephone lines all the way up the mountain. It seems to be climbing a series of giant steps in bedrock. At 1 mile, it levels out, then climbs again to the bare summit. You will find the nearly bare summit has views almost as good as those from the tower, and it is covered in summer with blueberries and chokecherries. The summit with its windmill, generator, broadcasting antennae, and helicopter pad is something of a disappointment.

Another winter snowshoe trek involves a two car shuttle. Climb the cliffs on Little Cathead, continue northeast across its summit, descending, and climbing again, still to the northeast to a middle summit in the Cathead range. Cliffs to the northeast of this summit make descent in this direction impossible, but you can descend northwest for 200 feet into the saddle. From here a route of due north leads up Cathead. Snowshoers find that descending via an old service road that lies east of the main Cathead trail is easiest. That route is too overgrown with brambles for summer use. It reaches almost to the level area, 200 feet below Cathead's summit.

90 Groff Creek
Old road, walking, hiking

River Road follows the west side of the Sacandaga River, north from the Benson Road. It is black-topped for a short distance, then becomes a hard-packed gravel road. It passes through private and posted lands but with its proximity to the river, it is pleasant for walking or even bicycling.

Park 4.7 miles north at the end of the dirt road, at a sign advising that the road has been abandoned and that you proceed at your own risk. The road is bordered with patches of private lands, but it is an old public right-of-way leading to Forest Preserve lands.

Cross Petes Creek on an old broken bridge and after about 0.2 mile, take a right fork in the road. Shortly beyond the road ends. Follow the continuing footpath straight ahead, as it climbs and angles west along a level section of Groff Creek, which is down below on your right. At a fork five minutes later, stay left. The old roadway circles southwest, then south, climbing nearly 400 feet up the northern flanks of Groff Mountain on a spectacularly steep traverse of those flanks. The road, built before 1850, represents an extraordinary construction feat. The slopes below are hemlock shrouded and lovely. Less than thirty minutes past the fork you see the first of two waterfalls on the creek. Beyond the second, less than ten minutes later, the creek quiets down, and in another ten minutes reaches a marsh over which you have views of Wallace Mountain. The hour-and-a-quarter walk to this marsh, 2.2 miles, is a lovely ramble through deep forest with numerous views of the creek.

91 Toward King Vly
Bushwhack

The stream that flows from the draw southeast of King Vly heads generally east and flows into Groff Creek where the latter loops north. The new metric USGS is wrong at this point. As soon as the streams join, they split, flowing parallel for 300 yards before they rejoin to plunge steeply down to the Sacandaga River. The whole valley is forested with large hemlocks that shade out any understory to make walking through the forest a delight.

Heading out from the path toward Groff Creek, section 90, take the right footpath, which itself splits in a hundred feet. Right leads to the split Groff Creek and if you cross here you can enjoy the wonderful bushwhack on high ground to the north of the creek to the confluence. (A draw that forms to the north of this raised bench may account for the mapmakers error. A small stream in that draw does lead northeast into the Sacandaga.) Alternatively, the left path leads to within fifty feet of the confluence of the streams. Once you are sure you have the branch from the draw below King Vly, follow it upstream through a relatively level valley for half a mile or more.

A road beside the stream was used to haul lumber from the interior before 1870, but cliffs at the head of the draw were so steep that the roadway had to be protected by hemlock bows in order to reduce ice and make the trip safe for horse-drawn sleighs. Stories of such a covered roadway induced me to explore the valley and on a recent trip we found a built up section of the road at the head of the draw.

The cliffs and slopes sheltering the valley are wonderfully steep, but without summer views. Those to the north, on a shoulder of Southerland Mountain, are strewn with rocks and rubble as if they were a raw road-cut and not a remnant of the glacier. In summer the valley is filled with mosquitoes and horse nettles and a walk through would be a disaster if this were not the southernmost place where the rare Braun's Holly Fern can be found. The valley beside the creek is level at first, but as the valley narrows, walking becomes very rough. As you begin to climb, look for the built-up road bed to the south of the creek. Allow about two hours to reach the place the draw turns to the northwest, more if you want to challenge this wild and remote valley.

The Mayfield Hills

IN THE LATE 1700s settlers pushed into the gently rolling hills north of the Mohawk to cultivate fields from Johnstown to Fish House on the Sacandaga. Northwest of the flood plain of the Sacandaga, the Mayfield Hills were their sentinel, guarding the lowlands, signaling the boundaries of their homesteads, and marking the borders of the distant impenetrable wilderness.

The Mayfield Hills continue to mark the southeastern boundary of the Adirondack wilds. Most of the land on the hills is now privately owned, but four adventures beckon hikers. A route to the cliffs behind Gifford Valley was included in previous editions. The access is currently posted and some development is planned, especially across from the access point along Woodward Lake. It is hoped that access to the hillside will be included in future plans so that hikers can once again enjoy this cliff that overlooks the Great Sacandaga Lake. Two routes are new, the result of trail planning by Fulton County. They are snowmobile routes that bring both hiking and skiing possibilities.

92 Jackson Summit West Road
Snowmobile trail, hiking, skiing, birding
5.4 miles, 2½ hours, 200-foot elevation change

A very old dirt road starts at the Gloversville City Reservoir and heads north beside several wetlands, ending at Tomantown Road and Hartwell Swamp, an excellent place for birding. The road connects with the trail of section 94.

Take Jackson Summit Road northwest from NY 30 north of Mayfield and turn north on Jackson Summit West Road. In winter, the snowmobile trail begins 0.3 mile north of this intersection; it crosses the outlet of the Gloversville (Jackson Summit) Reservoir and continues along the dirt road which is passable in summer for a mile or two (three or more with four-wheel-drive vehicles).

The road passes that reservoir on the west and at 2 miles passes the turn-off to a second reservoir. There is a hunting club at 3 miles and just beyond a vly on the right. At 3.2 miles, the road begins to climb, around the shoulder of Lawyer Mountain, traversing it in deep woods. Then, there

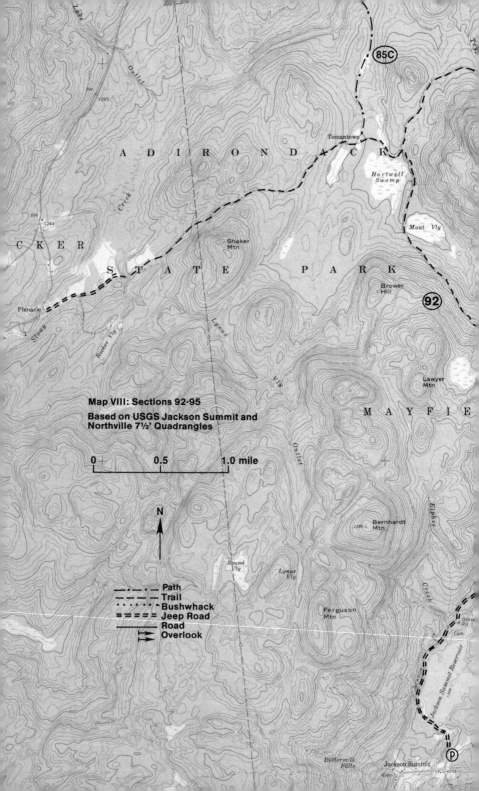

85C

Tomantown

ADIRONDACK

Hartwell
Swamp

Moat Vly

Shaker
Mtn

CKER

STATE   PARK

Brower
Hill

92

Pinnacle

Rocker Vly

Lawyer
Mtn

MAYFIE

Map VIII: Sections 92-95

Based on USGS Jackson Summit and
Northville 7½' Quadrangles

|0   0.5   1.0 mile|

N

Bernhardt
Mtn

Round
Vly

Lynus
Vly

Ferguson
Mtn

Cem

—·—·—·— Path
– – – – Trail
············ Bushwhack
▪▪▪▪▪▪ Jeep Road
————— Road
→→→ Overlook

Buttermilk
Falls

Jackson Summit

P

is a long, gentle descent over an occasionally water-rutted track to the outlet of Moat Vly at 4.9 miles. Loggers have been active north of this point. The trail is now east of Hartwell Swamp. At 5.4 miles it intersects the trail of section 94. Turn left for 200 yards to the outlet of Hartwell Swamp for birds and views of mountains to the south.

93 Feldspar Mine
Bushwhack along old road, hiking, snowshoeing

In the late 1800s and early 1900s, feldspar was mined in the Mayfield Hills and shipped to factories in New Jersey where it was ground to a very fine powder and used as a glaze for china. Also in the late 1800s, the Fonda, Johnstown, and Gloversville Railroad was extended to Northampton, a resort town now mostly flooded by the Great Sacandaga Lake. A long conveyor belt was built from the feldspar mine on the Mayfield Hills to the railroad. Most of the old railroad route is now flooded by the lake, which was constructed as a reservoir. The conveyor belt has been removed and even the cut for the mine is hidden from view.

The mine site, an amphitheater of pink rock, remains and can be reached by bushwhacking along abandoned roads. To reach the mine, look for Mountain Road that forks west from NY 30 about 2 miles north of Mayfield. You will find an abandoned sand pit 3.5 miles north on Mountain Road, on the west side. At the head of the sand pit is an abandoned logging road, which intersects several other abandoned logging roads on the side of an unnamed hill in the Mayfield chain. One of these is the most direct route to the mine, and with care it can be followed for the 0.8-mile, 660-foot climb to the abandoned feldspar mine.

From the pit, the road heads northwest, following a creek. Then, in a small meadow, it turns southwest to round the mountain. There are several other logging roads, all less obvious, branching out at different points from the meadow. One heads north from the meadow and crosses the creek. Follow this one for 300 yards until it intersects another well-defined road. This was the original road to the mine and the land to the east, downhill, along it is posted. Use this road to continue northwest uphill.

Notice the deep ravine of the creek below on your left. Notice also the cement pillars that used to be stanchions for the cable that carried feldspar to the railroad. Just beyond, you will see the excavated area. Walls of pink orthoclase feldspar rim the basin. The beautiful pink circular wall drips with dark green mosses, kept moist by the stream flowing through the mine. The mine is at the head of the draw below the summit of the mountain. The exposed coarse-grained igneous rock also contains other feldspars, micas, and quartz, showing glacial striations.

The mine was worked into the 1920s and supplied ore to a "modern" gravity-fed mill near Cranberry Creek in the vicinity of the present NY 30. When you return to that road, look in the field east of the Old Red Barn Airport where a huge conical pile of tailings accumulated beside the railroad right-of-way.

94 Extension of Warner Hill Road
Snowmobile trail, hiking
3.5 miles, 2 hours, 500-foot elevation change

Warner Hill Road turns west from Mountain Road 4.3 miles north of NY 30. The road leads in 0.6 mile to an intersection; the way straight is the route of the snowmobile trail, the way left leads in 300 yards to a deep green reservoir at the base of a deep and very handsome hemlock gorge. The way right is a connector for the snowmobile trail that passes Woodward Lake. Parking is severely limited, so pull off to the side and do not block any of the continuing routes.

The trail/roadway climbs very steeply west along the small stream that drains what once was the Sacandaga Park Reservoir. You reach that reservoir, now shallow because the dam is out, in 1 mile. The trail becomes level in a tall pine plantation, descends briefly, turns southeast to climb again, then heads east to join the Tomantown Road. That roadway follows high above the south banks of Trypoli Creek to the northwest, curves around the north flanks of Steele Mountain, and becomes drivable again as it reaches the logging lands owned by Finch Pruyn Company. At 3.3 miles you reach the intersection with the snowmobile trail from the south, section 92, and at 3.5 miles you see Hartwell Swamp.

Note that this roadway continues past a point on the map called Tomantown and on for nearly 3 miles to Pinnacle on the Stony Creek. It is drivable for most of this distance and heavily used by logging trucks. While this section makes a good winter route for snowmobiles and has great potential for skiers, its summer use is limited. The route is not currently posted, but has been in the past.

95 Mud Lake and Overlook Cliff
Bushwhack

This relatively difficult bushwhack begins from Warner Hill Road, which is a left, west, turn from Mountain Road, 4.3 miles north of NY 30. Park as indicated in section 94 and walk 50 yards along the extension of the road, crossing the small creek, to a small field on the north side of the snowmobile trail. This field is the beginning of the bushwhack to Mud Lake.

This bushwhack is difficult because there are no landmarks. You will have to follow a compass course toward magnetic north for over 0.7 mile to reach Mud Lake. The bushwhack should take between forty-five minutes and an hour. The compass route takes you steeply up a little over 600 feet, around the northeast side of a small knob, then down 75 feet in elevation to lake level.

Mud Lake is a bog and is good for studying typical bog flora, when it is not flooded by beaver. There are remnants of a logging road around the far (northern) side, which you can use to walk around the lake.

On your return, climb to the knob and drop down to ledges that face the south side, 0.3 mile south of the lake. From these ledges there is a fine view of Great Sacandaga Lake and Tamarack Swamp below. Now descend east of south to reach the valley and Warner Hill Road again.

The West Branch and Whitehouse

As early as 1835, settlers pushed west of the Sacandaga Valley to harvest the rich timber in the valley beside the West Branch of the Sacandaga, or the West River as it has always been known to natives. Several mills were constructed on the river to handle logs that were floated from as far away as Piseco and Arietta.

Today, the stretch of dirt and gravel road beside the West River is the only road into the wilderness of the West Branch spiral, and it offers a handsome introduction to the deep interior. Its destination, 9 miles from NY 30, was the Whitehouse, a hunting and fishing camp. Log cabins surrounded a main house, but only the stone fireplaces remain. Drive the length of the road, stroll from its end along the West Branch, and become acquainted with the edge of the Adirondacks' deepest wilderness.

The trip to Whitehouse on the narrow road is an adventure in itself, even though it passes in part through land that has been recently logged. Just south of the village of Wells on NY 30, Algonquin Drive heads west and crosses the outlet of Lake Algonquin within sight of the dam that creates the lake from the Main Branch of the Sacandaga. West River Road forks left or south from Algonquin Drive, 0.7 mile from NY 30, and continues southwest to Blackbridge, at 2.4 miles.

From Blackbridge west, the road is narrow and driving speeds of twenty miles an hour are sufficient. Between Blackbridge and Jimmy Creek, the road is close to the river with great vistas across the rushing water and standing waves to the mountains that form this deep and scenic part of the gorge. At 3.5 miles there is a turnout to a picnic spot beside the river.

At just over 4 miles there is a new bridge over Jimmy Creek. Park nearby. There is a delightful picnic spot beside the old ford just west of the bridge. Beyond Jimmy Creek there is a steep hill where West River Road can be especially bad early in the season before crews have regraded it. From Jimmy Creek to Whitehouse, the road is above and out of sight of the river, much of the time through private land.

At 6.8 miles, a pair of roads, both currently posted, lead to the West River in the vicinity of Ninemile Creek. Because of this posting, descriptions given in previous editions are omitted from this guide. You reach Forest Preserve land at 7.3 miles, the river is way below in a deep gorge at this point. Near Dugway Brook at 7.5 miles there are several lovely camp-sites. At 8.5 miles you reach the open fields that once surrounded White-house. Here, you find several lovely approaches to the river and campsites and fireplaces and chimneys from the old buildings.

Between Wells and Whitehouse, the West Branch falls 300 feet as it tumbles through many sections of pretty rapids. Near Whitehouse and to the west, the river flows through a broader, flatter valley with two large, quiet eddies. Farther west are rapids and falls where the stream drops over 200 feet in a mile. This segment is described in sections 98 and 100.

Whitehouse is in a lovely, broad, upland valley with Dugway Mountain rising dramatically to the northeast. It provides an inviting center for all sorts of activities, especially hiking. The Northville-Placid Trail crosses the West Branch near Whitehouse on an enormous suspension bridge. Fishermen and campers find adequate parking here, and hikers will find it is the best jumping off place for the interior of the Silver Lake Wilderness.

Winter travelers should note that the road is plowed only to within 2 miles of Whitehouse. While skiers and snowshoers can enjoy the road, the additional 2 miles make it very difficult for each of the destinations described in this chapter, except as winter backpacking trips.

South of Wells, at the Sacandaga Campground, the West Branch joins the main stream of the Sacandaga River, which continues to flow south, visible much of the way from NY 30. Along the river there are several picnic grounds and campsites, both private and public. With advance planning, hikers should be able to find accommodations in the area or locate a campsite suitable for enjoying the several walks in this chapter.

96 Jimmy Creek
Path, walking, fishing

Jimmy Creek tumbles over 400 feet in 0.8 mile from the end of the long valley between Mount Dunham and Hamilton Mountain into the West Branch, which it meets 1.6 miles west of Blackbridge. Its lovely series of small falls and cataracts and sparkling clear water are punctuated by a deep chute through folded rock ledges and a surprising waterfall that drops forty feet over a horizontally tiered headwall. The creek is secreted in a deep valley protected by towering hemlocks.

Photographers would enjoy the lower creek best before midday when sunlight can filter into the southeast-flowing water. Except for a short period in late morning, the creek lies in deep shade.

Park at the turnout west of the bridge over Jimmy Creek. A faint path leads along the east side of Jimmy Creek through a parcel recently acquired by the state. Follow the path upstream or hop rocks on the shore for better views when the path swings back from the water.

It will take twenty minutes to walk to the beautiful sluice and another ten minutes to reach the deep pool below the falls. Note that the path is safely away from the tumbling water. It could be dangerous near the falls. The path climbs east around the falls to the ravine above and becomes increasingly faint as far as a sharp bend in the creek. You can reach the bend after forty-five minutes of walking from the road, but no one would walk that fast—there is far too much to enjoy!

Beyond the bend, the creek levels out and is less dramatic, but it still has good, deep woods on either side. You can either walk along the rocks in the creek or back in the high, open hemlock groves where witch hobble fills the forest floor. All signs of the path are gone, but even after it disappears, the walking is easy.

Boulders in the creek are tinged with the pink of feldspar and an occasional rock is studded with garnet. Near the falls, sheer ledges are green and dripping with moss. On the return, notice the strange rock formation beside the pool below the falls. It is man-made, an old rock diversion wall to steer logs downstream below the falls. It is hard to imagine that this remote stream was ever used to float logs to mills below.

Jimmy Creek is too splendid for all but the most leisurely visit. The climb beside it is so gentle that most people can enjoy the walk to the falls, one of the most brilliant gems in the southern Adirondacks.

97 Finch Mountain Cliffs
Bushwhack

Finch Mountain has the only views in the West Branch Valley, but reaching its cliffs involves a difficult bushwhack and access to the mountain depends on low water in the river. If these deterrents can be overcome, the result is an exciting adventure, for the cliffs are high enough and so exposed you have an eagle's perspective of the long West Branch Valley.

Park near the bridge over Jimmy Creek, 1.6 miles west of Blackbridge. Below and to the west is a log-based ford. The ford is too slippery for easy walking, even in very low water. Just upstream you can find a place where low water rock hopping is possible. Perhaps you should carry your hiking boots and wear an old pair of boots or sneakers for the trip across the river. Note that in spring or in high water, this sort of crossing is *impossible*. The West Branch is far too big a river and too much water flows over its rocks to make crossing safe except for a short time each summer. When the water is high, the current is too swift for a safe canoe or boat crossing. So, wait for a dry spell and then plan to take this trip. And, before you start, you may want to study the cliffs from a view spot on West River Road, 2.3 miles west of Jimmy Creek. This view will help you plan the trip as no description can.

Finch is a small cone-shaped mountain that rises 900 feet in a little over 0.5 mile from the river. After crossing the river, select a compass heading of 210° magnetic. This route traverses the steep northwestern face of the mountain toward the summit. For the first 300 feet the climb is very steep and difficult, requiring the use of hands to scramble over the duff-covered talus, which provides poor footing. Only a long trek from the east would avoid the scramble, so persevere. Above the first 300 feet, the climb is more gradual with huge glacial erratic blocks strewn across the gentler slopes. You will find that a few of the enormous erratics are quite remarkable.

Below the summit and to the west there is a series of small cliffs you can get around in order to reach the outcrops with the best views. However, it is easier simply to go over the summit and descend 40 feet to reach them. You may encounter several small cliff tops before reaching the best one, from which there is a splendid view stretching from Dunham, Cutknife, Speculator, and Hamilton mountains to the north, past Dugway and Swart and the West Branch Valley to Three Sisters Mountain in the distant west. Ninemile Creek Valley is clearly defined cutting through the ridge that borders the West Branch Valley to the south.

The round trip bushwhack can be made in three hours. This does not offer ample time to enjoy the views. The return can be fairly easily directed, and it is best to retrace your steps. Watch the ledges along the last 300 feet on the return to the river. And, again, do not attempt the trip at all if water in the West Branch is not sufficiently low to provide a safe crossing.

Jimmy Creek Waterfalls

98 Walk along the West River
Path, hiking, camping

From the west end of the parking field at the end of West River Road, a path along the continuing, but gated roadway leads in 250 yards to a registration booth at the Northville-Placid Trail. The way right is described in sections 80, 100, and 101. The way left is the trail described in section 99. However, if you cross the big suspension bridge whose northern end begins near the fireplace that is all that remains of the old Whitehouse lodge, you will find an unmarked path that follows the river west for almost a mile before it peters out. It passes several remote campsites near the water, sheltered by tall hemlock. Use this route if you have only time for a short getaway, use the next section if you have time for an extended trip.

99 Canary Pond and Silver Lake
8.4 miles, 4 ½ hours, 800-foot elevation change

The walk from Whitehouse south to Canary Pond and on to Silver Lake passes through marvelously rugged woods, the best forest cover along the entire length of the Northville-Placid Trail. Most people use the lean-tos at Mud Pond and Silver Lake to break up a backpacking trip from Benson, section 83, north to Whitehouse or Piseco. If, like me, you prefer a trip without a pack, try this as a one-day walk and return, possibly going only as far as Canary Pond. Better yet, consider a nine-hour trek from Whitehouse to Benson; this is among the best of the one-day wilderness hikes in the Adirondacks. Most of the land south of Whitehouse has been owned by the State since the 1880s; it was logged but only hemlock and spruce were cut and the logging was a very light one that took only very large trees. As a result, the forest has returned to old-growth proportions.

From the sign-in booth at Whitehouse, 0.15 mile from the parking fields, head south across the marvelous suspension bridge and into a superb forest of hemlock and spruce. Within ten minutes you cross a little stream and make a sharp turn right where a path leads left back to the river. Climbing gently, the trail reaches a draw and briefly follows a stream, crossing it at 1.65 miles. A beautiful uphill traverse leads to a height-of-land at just over 2 miles. A gentle descent, two more small stream crossings, and impressive hemlock forests lead you downhill at 3.1 miles to the reconstructed lean-to at Mud Lake.

Map IX: Sections 96-97, 102-104
Based on USGS Lake Pleasant 15' Quadrangle

Circling Mud Pond around the west and south sides, the trail crosses at Noisy Brook at 3.8 miles, then angles south again to traverse the lower flanks of Moose Mountain, in a tall hardwood forest. A stream appears downslope on your left; you cross it a feeder stream, then the main brook at 5.15 miles at your approach to a large beaver dam that has created a pretty meadow ringed with huge spruce and hemlock. A muddy detour walk around the vly leads to a narrow path uphill that rejoins the older route. After a gentle uphill through more spectacular forest, the trail winds south skirting several marshy areas before descending to Canary Pond at 6.4 miles.

The trail is back from the marshy shores of Canary Pond, where the trail makes a right angle turn to the east to continue past more marshes, across a small bridge, uphill, then past more marshes with lovely views. The trail turns south again to descend to the lean-to at Silver Lake's southeastern corner.

100 Falls on the West Branch Sacandaga
Bushwhack

Of all the walks into the wilderness bordered by the West Branch, this one is certainly the most dramatic, with some of the most wonderful scenery in the Adirondacks. Much can be said of the West Branch and its many moods, most of which are expressed in this one walk. The river is quiet by Big Eddy, fierce through the rapids and the gorge beside the falls, and then hidden and mysterious beneath towering cliffs.

No matter what the weather or the time of year, it is a long and difficult walk. In early spring when the river is its wildest, the trip to the falls is almost impossible. In midsummer, when the water is low, the stream is less exciting, but the walking is easier. The rugged tumbles of boulders are certainly enhanced by large flows of water, but the impressive scenery is not totally dependent on them.

The trip to the falls begins west of Whitehouse and follows the Northville-Placid Trail northwest for 0.8 mile to a fork. The way right, which heads north, is the continuing Northville-Placid Trail and is well marked. The left fork is a path that follows an abandoned logging road west for 0.6 mile to Hamilton Lake Stream. The route is very wide, flat, and easy to walk.

West Branch of the Sacandaga River above Whitehouse

Hamilton Lake Stream is a principal cause of the difficulties on this walk. The cable bridge over the stream has been gone for some time. In high water, the crossing can be wet. In low water, though, you can hop across on exposed rocks. With no definite route across the stream, hikers have taken a variety of routes on the west side so that no one clear footpath is obvious. If you can find one follow it southwest toward the river. If you cannot find one, just head southwest, knowing you will intersect the river in 200 yards.

Your first glimpse of the eddies on the river is so lovely you will wish the path had been closer to the river all the way west from Whitehouse. Beyond, upstream, it stays by the water's edge for nearly 1 mile, past the first eddy, a series of rapids, then Big Eddy, and on to the outlet of Cold Brook. In the last 0.5 mile, the route is but a fisherman's path, for no road ever extended this far. Cold Brook has the distinction of a stand of poison ivy—that scourge that is generally absent from the Adirondacks.

From Cold Brook west, the valley narrows so that in places steep cliffs rise directly from the river bed. The path at first clings to the steep shore, then almost disappears, so that it seems easier to hop along rocks at the water's edge. After the first big bend with its deep pool and cliffs on the south, it is definitely easier, in low water, to walk along the edge of the river.

In the 0.5 mile west of Cold Brook there is no quiet water; a crescendo of rapids leads to the first falls. Behind the falls, cliffs on the north shore rise 200 feet above the river. On their crests are huge white pines, which make the cliffs seem even taller. If you look back east along the rapids, you will see many of these huge pines dotting the shoreline.

You can climb, with some difficulty, around the boulders on the north side of the falls to reach the second falls, only 200 yards upstream. The trek between the falls is so difficult that it can take as much as forty-five minutes. Although the beauty of the second falls justifies the trip, it is recommended for only the most agile and prudent. In high water, it is necessary to climb the cliffs to continue along the river.

The second falls are even narrower and higher than the first, and both are pretty, even in low water. The enormous boulders that line the gorge attest to nature's past violence, but there are signs of recent furies. Perhaps you can spot the shattered hulk of an old rowboat fifteen feet high on a rock ledge. It underscores the temper of the river and illustrates the vast amount of water it carries and the huge area it drains.

There are few difficulties encountered on the return trip that are not met on the outward walk, with the exception of tired feet and legs. With time to rest and picnic and photograph, you can easily spend six hours on this hike.

101 West Branch Gorge
Difficult bushwhack, camping

The pair of waterfalls on the West Branch 3 miles west of Whitehouse stand at the eastern edge of the deepest part of the river's gorge, with formidable cliffs deterring travel farther west. Tales of another waterfall tempted me to explore the hidden recesses of the wild river. In the years since the first edition of this guide appeared, I have walked many places in the Adirondacks and explored routes for several more guides, but no trip was as wonderful as the walk through the West Branch Gorge, where I discovered not one, but three more waterfalls. A bushwhack along the river is as challenging and exciting as any you might attempt. I recommend this route as a one-day through-trek, starting at Whitehouse early in the morning. You will complete the bushwhack just before nightfall, coming out on NY 10 via the path along Piseco Outlet, section 77.

In high water much of the trip has to be walked on the edge of the gorge, too far back or high up to appreciate the river. Only in very low water is it possible to hop rocks and follow the river's course between eddies and falls.

Since the river falls 300 vertical feet in a distance of 2 miles, it might seem prudent to walk downstream, but I prefer walking upstream, approaching the river's waterfalls from below. There are truly beautiful places to camp on the trip through, and the length of the trip makes camping desirable. The best camping place is at the second pair of falls.

Beyond the first pair of falls, section 100, the river tumbles through a dark-walled ravine where even at noon the deep green of overhanging hemlock and pines brings dusk to the river. A series of deep pools accompany you 0.3 mile west, and then the river makes a big bend to the southwest. Here the channel is so narrow and strong that it may be necessary to climb out of the gorge, even in low water.

The third waterfall appears as the river banks become less steep. When you first spot the third falls, look sharply, for the fourth is hiding scarcely 200 yards upstream from it. There is a deep pool below each. The walls beside the pool above the third falls make traveling so difficult that you will need almost forty-five minutes to walk between the two falls; even more time and agility than is required for the trip between the first pair of falls.

On the bank on the north shore above the fourth falls, a marvelous campsite is obviously well used. It is high on a hemlock protected ledge covered

with a deep cushion of moss and creeping white winterberry. A rudimentary path leads west from the campsite along the river.

Above the fourth falls, there is another beautiful eddy, and above it, a fifth cataract, just west of the outlet of Owl Pond. Hunter's paths can be found on the north shore of the river west of the eddy. Beyond the westernmost rapids, the river is broad and there are no more paths on the north shore. Walking along it is very difficult, for it is rimmed with a dense alder swamp. Paths make walking on the south shore a bit easier; however, they end before you reach the confluence of the West Branch and Piseco Outlet. Without a canoe, the only way out is to swim the river in the quiet water near the confluence. If you can cross the river and reach the west shore of Piseco Outlet, it is a simple matter to pick up the extension of the confluence path, section 77, and use it to reach NY 10.

If the thought of swimming the West Branch does not appeal to you, make your way along the north shore to Piseco Outlet and upstream along the outlet to the area of the islands, where it is possible to ford that stream. Rough going should be anticipated in the alders beside the river; unfortunately walking back from its border is little better.

Allow three hours for the walk from Whitehouse to the first pair of waterfalls, an hour and a half for the walk to the second pair, an hour to reach Owl Pond outlet, less than an hour for the trek to the last cataract, an hour for the walk along the south shore of the flow to the Piseco Outlet confluence, and an hour and a half to swim the river and walk out to NY 10. This total of nine hours is easily extended to ten or more to allow time for lunch and photographs. Walking is so difficult in places that distances do not convey a true sense of the difficulty involved. You will travel at least 7 miles on the bushwhack. This remote adventure through a valley whose grandeur is unrivaled in the southern Adirondacks is extraordinarily difficult, a fact that will leave the gorge untouched and unspoiled for years to come.

102 Near the Confluence of the West and Main Branches of the Sacandaga

Dirt roads, walking, cross-country skiing

Walking along little traveled dirt roads can be the best way to watch for birds and enjoy the scenery. Two sections of roads south of Wells are ideal.

West Branch of the Sacandaga River above Whitehouse

Drive southwest from Wells to Blackbridge and cross the river. The road straight ahead, south, is heavily posted, but a left turn, to the east, takes you on a dirt road that ends on a loop in the Wilderness Area. The road is adjacent to the West Branch, but out of sight of it and leads to a point opposite the Sacandaga Campground. In summer it offers birds, berries, and butterflies. In winter it offers a chance for easy cross-country skiing. The road reaches state land within 1 mile of Blackbridge, then makes a loop just over 1 mile long. A short side path to Vly Creek leaves the road 400 yards before the easternmost part of the loop.

Even prettier is the 1.5-mile walk along the dirt surfaced section of the road on the west side of the Main Branch of the Sacandaga south of Wells. Cross the outlet of Lake Algonquin and take the first left turn to the south. Park beyond the surfaced road. No matter the weather, walking close to the Sacandaga is thrilling: colorful in autumn, quiet in summer, wild in the late winter or early spring, when showshoes or cross-country skis may be necessary. You can walk all the way to Sacandaga Campground, which lies just south of the end of the road.

Gilmantown Road

AT THE END of the eighteenth century, settlers began to move to the community of Wells on the Main Branch of the Sacandaga and build saw mills to harvest the rich timber in the surrounding mountains. Today the hills around Lake Algonquin bear the names of the early settlers, the Overackers, who were among the first; Petit, for years a hotelkeeper in the community; and the Dunhams.

A road existed from Wells north to Lake Pleasant as early as 1805, but the War of 1812 saw the designing of the "Old Military Road" from Albany to Sacketts Harbor, on the shores of Lake Ontario. The road went through the communities of Northville and Hope to Wells. At Wells, it headed northwest beside Elbow Creek, and past Charley and Mud lakes to the outlet of Lake Pleasant. Beyond Lake Pleasant, the road headed through Wilcox Clearing to follow the Miami and Cedar rivers, and approached Raquette Lake. The course was said to be along an old Indian trail and the road was supposed to have been laid out with "considerable engineering skill." The portion of the road north of Lake Pleasant had grown to brush and was impassable except on foot as early as 1820.

The road from Wells to Lake Pleasant, known as the Gilmantown Road, was an important highway link and was the principal route north until the end of the nineteenth century. A parallel route, now called "Old Route 30," was begun in 1862 along the Sacandaga Valley, but it did not supplant the Gilmantown Road until this century.

In 1835, David Dunning acquired the land around the pond east of Gilmantown Road that bears his name. He built a sawmill there and operated it through the 1860s.

When gold rush fever hit the Adirondacks in the 1880s, prospectors claimed to have found gold on Elbow Creek and a mine shaft was dug. Gold and silver were never mined successfully, but countless companies sold shares and were organized to seek out the precious metals everyone thought had to be in the mountains.

Today the Gilmantown Road invites hikers to several adventures. Each adventure would be enhanced by reading the chapter on Wells in Aber and King's *The History of Hamilton County,* from which these background notes on the Gilmantown Road were taken.

To find the road, drive north on NY 30, 0.25 mile past the bridge over the Sacandaga at the north end of Lake Algonquin and the community of Wells. Gilmantown Road is a left turn from NY 30. The road leads up the hill between Mount Overrocker and Pettit Mountain. Part of the land beside Elbow Creek is posted, but there are several clearly marked sections of Forest Preserve land where you might wish to stop for a picnic.

103 Pettit Mountain Cliffs

Easy bushwhack, hiking, picnicking

Drive north of NY 30 on Gilmantown Road for 1.5 miles. Here the road crosses Elbow Creek. The east shore is posted but 200 yards south, opposite two distinctive boulders edging the west side of the road, Elbow Creek is clearly marked as state land. From this point, it is possible to make a very steep but rewarding climb to the cliffs on Pettit Mountain.

The route is generally east up the face of the mountain. The first 200 feet or so to the power line are precipitous but not dangerous. Continue past the power line, climbing until the lower cliffs are visible. The easiest route is to the right, south, around the cliffs.

You will reach a shelf from which there are several vantage points. Continue northeast across the shelf to the second range of cliffs. Walk north, left, beyond the cliffs before attempting to scale them to the summit. The entire summit area is steep, but the cliffs on the south face are too vertical to scale. At that you will find you have to scramble to attain the summit from the northwest.

Cross the spruce-covered summit to the exposed ledges on the south. Overactive campers have done some damage to the summit and cleared walkways through the spruce cover.

The views are fantastic, up Elbow Creek Valley toward Speculator Mountain; west to Hamilton, Cutknife, and Round mountains; across Lake Algonquin and the Sacandaga Valley to Cathead, Wallace, and Three Ponds mountains in the southwest; and east to the range of small hills with cliffs beyond the Sacandaga to Hadley and Roundtop on the distant horizon.

The cliffs are high! Stay back from the edge. Return with care, retracing the route to avoid dangerous ledges. The climb, 400 feet in a little more than 0.25 mile, will seem incredibly steep, but commensurate with the rewards for the forty-five minutes of bushwhack climbing. The return can be made in twenty minutes.

104 Dunning Pond

Hiking
4.3 miles, 2½ hours, 550-foot elevation change

This trail marked for snowmobiles runs from Gilmantown Road past Dunning Pond, along the pond's outlet, and then through the woods on a newly cut route to an old logging road that intersects NY 30 just north of Dunning Creek. Both the eastern and western parts of the trail follow old logging roads.

The eastern terminus of the trail is on NY 30 just 0.3 mile south of the NY 8 bridge over the Sacandaga. To find the western trailhead, drive 0.5 mile north of Charley Lake. This point is 0.2 mile south of the bridge over Dunning Creek.

The trail follows a course generally east from Gilmantown Road for 0.9 mile toward Dunning Pond, contouring around the hills south of the pond. Growth conceals the pond that lies but 100 yards north of the trail. Watch as the trail swings south near the outlet, you will come to the easiest access to the pond. There are signs of an old road, a stone bridge, and foundations on a spruce-covered rise between the trail and the outlet. This is the site of the mill operated by David Dunning in the middle of the nineteenth century. Now the pond is nearly dry meadow filling with swampy shrubs.

The next 1.5 miles are lovely, for the route is close to the south shore of the creek. The beautiful woods and high mixed forest with some outstanding hemlock shelter a rich understory of ferns and mosses. The outlet has a few little rapids interspersed with deep pools, and there is one small waterfall.

The trail along the south side of the stream is poorly marked but easy to follow, with a few wet places to traverse. You will reach a washed out snowmobile bridge at the end of a stillwater, and 0.2 mile from the bridge the creek begins to fall steeply toward NY 30.

You can follow the trail to the old logging road, which descends to NY 30, although the newly cut part is difficult to find because of inadequate marking. It heads due north from the creek, climbing the hillside to intersect the old road. The road winds downhill toward NY 30 through good, mixed hardwood forest, and walking this section is pleasant. The creek is below, south, of the logging road, deep in the hemlock-covered ravine and out of sight of the road. You can hear it in one or two places near NY 30, but most of the time it is disappointingly far away. The section from the snowmobile bridge to NY 30 is slightly circuitous and covers 2 miles in a descent of almost 700 feet to the highway.

The trip described so far assumes that you have arranged to have cars at both ends. There is an even better way to enjoy the creek. On the first day, with one car, walk from Gilmantown Road to the bridge and back, and make a second trip up from NY 30 to the washed out bridge on the second day. Then, instead of retracing your steps on the logging road, follow the creek to NY 30. Of course, this is easiest to do in low water.

East of the snowmobile bridge, the creek begins a precipitous drop with the most beautiful rock slides and small pools. The upper part is a dramatic series of small falls and lovely boulders. Sometimes you can hop rocks in the stream bed; sometimes you will have to improvise a route beside the creek. Pick the early part of a bright blue day for a walk down the creek and be rewarded by a tapestry of multicolored reflecting pools below large shelves of boulder-strewn walls. The steep banks of the ravine that shelters the lower part of the creek keep it quiet and secluded, even as it approaches NY 30.

You will find the berry bulblet fern, *Cystopteris bulbiferous*, growing on ledges beside the stream near the highway. Their presence indicates limestone in the rocks.

If you walk through from Gilmantown Road to NY 30 following the trail all the way, you will need less than three hours. If you follow the trail to the bridge and then bushwhack along the creek, you can easily spend four hours on the trek. If you climb from NY 30 to the stream, you will need an hour and a quarter for the walk to the washed-out bridge. You can walk from here to Dunning Pond and back in two hours more. The trip down the creek and back to NY 30 will take at least two hours. No matter what way you approach the creek, you will have a full day's adventure.

Driving Trips

IT MAY SEEM inappropriate to mention a motorized trip in a trail guide; however, one of my greatest pleasures has been to escort older friends who can no longer enjoy a forest walk on drives into almost wilderness areas. There are several routes so remote that they substitute for very active hikes. All are on public roads. Any one of these would also make a good introduction for newcomers and set the stage for further explorations.

The most obvious route is along the Powley-Piseco Road, see the first chapter for details and mileages. You may want to detour to the East Canada Creek as described in sections 1 and 2. The drive north is lovely, and when you reach Brayhouse Brook, section 5, you have an ideal picnic spot. The bridge at Powley Place also has a beautiful vista, both up and down the North Branch. I have watched deer while standing on the bridge. Farther north the road is edged with sheer cliffs between East and West Notch mountains. Look carefully in the trees beside the road—you can expect to see owls.

NY 10 north of Pine Lake has its treasures, one being the beaver houses established near the road in a swamp, 0.2 mile from the intersection with NY 29A. The swamps north of here come almost to the road and with little effort ferns and other unusual plants are easy to see. At the first bend in the road, you can look into Stoner Lake Outlet and find, in August, a stand of Cardinal flowers. The walk to the gorge, section 53, is not too much to add to a driving trip.

The drive along NY 10 in Hamilton County is unrivaled in the Adirondacks. There are many places along it from which to see the West Branch of the Sacandaga. Many of the valley's pleasures are visible from the road. I happen to think that dawn is the best time to see the river. The combinations of mist and reflections and slanting light are spectacular. Fall colors are always best here.

In late summer you will enjoy the sight of dew-covered cobwebs glistening in the morning sun from the high branches of trees silhouetted against the softness of the fog-shrouded swamps. I have three favorite places to stop and enjoy the river and photograph. One is at the "second bridge" north of Arietta; both sides of the bridge over the river are perfectly framed with trees and hills so the reflections in the quiet river double the scene in perfect symmetry. Another is south of Trout Lake Mountain where the meadow is always filled with a riot of color in August. Stop where State Brook flows under the road. The third is south of Shaker Place where the road has been widened; here are the best places to view the flows along the West Branch.

An early autumn drive loop along both these roads is a blaze of red swamp maples that line the waterways.

East of Caroga Lake there are several dirt roads heading south from Benson Road. One, which is 2.8 miles from the intersection of Benson Road and NY 10, leads to the site of the oldest Catholic Church in Fulton County. In the cemetery near the site, there are not only many old headstones to delight historians, but there are also some of the largest blueberries to be found anywhere.

NY 30 commands many views across the lower Sacandaga. This stretch combined with a drive up the road to Whitehouse becomes a beautiful excursion. You could picnic along the West Branch near Jimmy Creek or at Whitehouse. Remember that the dirt road often erodes badly in late winter, so driving it in early spring before it has been regraded can be difficult. Roads south along the Sacandaga also make good driving excursions, section 102.

You will also want to drive north from Wells along Gilmantown Road. The Gilmantown Road chapter gives the brief history of that section. Stop along Elbow Creek for a picnic.

Every fall, you ought to enjoy a trip around the Big Horn as natives of the fringes of the Adirondacks call the trip up NY 30 from the Mohawk Valley, west on NY 8, and south on NY 10. You might question why the circular route is called a trip around the horn, but there is a logical explanation. At the very southern edge of the Adirondacks in the Town of Caroga, the Cape Horn Road follows the Caroga Creek after making a sharp angle with NY 29. That angle, which resembled the horn of South America, inspired the naming of the road. In the early twentieth century, a drive from Johnstown north to the edges of the mountains circling around the Cape Horn Road became a trip around the Little Horn. With the advent of automobiles and longer Sunday excursions, the drive north to Speculator and Piseco became the trip around the Big Horn.

References and Other Resources

References

Aber, Ted and Stella King, *The History of Hamilton County*. Lake Pleasant, NY: Great Wilderness Books, 1965.

McMartin, Barbara. *Caroga: The Town Recalls Its Past*. Caroga, NY: Town of Caroga, 1976.

Mickel, John T. *Ferns and Fern Allies*. Dubuque, Iowa: Wm. C. Brown Company Publishers, 1979.

Rickett, Harold William. *Wild Flowers of the United States: The Northeastern States*, Vol. 1. New York: The New York Botanical Garden and McGraw-Hill Book Company, 1966.

Sesquicentennial of the Town of Arietta, compiled in 1986, no title page, privately printed.

Simms, Jeptha R. *Trappers of New York, or a Biography of Nicholas Stoner and Nathaniel Foster*. Albany, NY: J. Munsell, 1857. Reprinted by Harbor Hill Books, 1980.

Williams, Donald R. *Oliver Whitman, Adirondack Guide and Other Stories*. Wells, NY: Haderondack House, 1979.

Other Resources

Adirondack Mountain Club, Glens Falls, NY, 12801

New York State Department of Environmental Conservation (DEC), 50 Wolf Road, Albany, NY 12233
DEC Region 5, Land and Forest Headquarters, Northville, NY 12134

For other things to do in the Adirondacks:
"I Love New York" series: *Camping, Tourism Map, State Travel Guide*. New York State Department of Commerce, Albany, New York, 12245

To find your way around the back roads:
Adirondack Region Atlas, City Street Directory, Poughkeepsie, New York. $3.75

For snowmobile and ski trails:
Snowmobiling in New York State, DEC booklet, available at all DEC offices

Arietta, Piseco, and Speculator Snowmobile and Ski Trail Map, available at local businesses and the Hamilton County Office of Tourism, Speculator

Fulton County Recreation Trails, four maps showing snowmobile and ski trails, Fulton County Planning Office, available at many local businesses

Index

Guidebooks from Backcountry Publications

For information on other regions of the Adirondacks covered in the "Discover" series, please see the back cover.

Walks & Rambles Series

Walks & Rambles in Dutchess and Putnam Counties, by PeggyTurco $10.95
Walks & Rambles in Rhode Island, by Ken Weber, Second Edition $11.00
More Walks & Rambles in Rhode Island, by Ken Weber $9.95
Walks & Rambles in the Upper Connecticut River Valley, by Mary L. Kibling $10.00
Walks & Rambles in Westchester (NY) and Fairfield (CT) Counties,
    by Katherine Anderson, revised by Peggy Turco, Second Edition $11.00
Walks &Rambles on Cape Cod and the Islands, by Ned Friary and Glenda Bendure $10.95
Walks & Rambles on the Delmarva Peninsula, by Jay Abercrombie $10.95

Hiking Series

Fifty Hikes in the Adirondacks, by Barbara McMartin, Second Edition $12.95
Fifty Hikes in Central New York, by William Ehling, $11.95
Fifty Hikes in Central Pennsylvania, by Tom Thwaites, Second Edition $10.95
Fifty Hikes in Connecticut, by Gerry and Sue Hardy, Third Edition $11.95
Fifty Hikes in Eastern Pennsylvania, by Carolyn Hoffman, Second Edition $12.00
Fifty Hikes in the Hudson Valley, by Barbara McMartin and Peter Kick $12.95
Fifty Hikes in Lower Michigan, by Jim DuFresne $13.00
Fifty Hikes in Massachusetts, by John Brady and Brian White, Second Edition $13.00
Fifty Hikes in New Jersey, by Bruce Scofield, Stella Green, and H. Neil
    Zimmerman $12.95
Fifty Hikes in Northern Maine, by Cloe Caputo $12.00
Fifty Hikes in Ohio, by Ralph Ramey $12.95
Fifty Hikes in Southern Maine, by John Gibson $10.95
Fifty Hikes in Vermont, by the Green Mountain Club, Fourth Edition $11.95
Fifty Hikes in Western New York, by William Ehling $13.00
Fifty HIkes in Western Pennsylvania, by Tom Thwaites, Second Edition $11.95
Fifty Hikes in the White Mountains, by Daniel Doan, Fourth Edition $12.95
Fifty More Hikes in New Hampshire, by Daniel Doan, Third Edition $12.95

We offer many more books on hiking, walking, fishing, and canoeing in the Midwest, New England, New York state, and the Mid-Atlantic states—plus books on travel, nature, and many other subjects.

Our titles are available in bookshops and in many sporting goods stores, or they may be ordered directly from the publisher. Shipping and handling costs are $2.50 for 1-2 books, $3 for 3-6 books, and $3.50 for 7 or more books. To order, or for a complete catalog, please write to The Countryman Press, Inc., P.O. Box 175, Dept. APC, Woodstock, VT 05091, or call our toll-free number, (800) 245-4151.

Stanford Pulrang grew up in Yonkers, New York, obtained a Masters Degree in Political Science from the University of Chicago, and worked for a decade at a bank in New York City and for two years at USAID in Vietnam. He then spent a year in the Yukon, followed by six years in British Columbia, where the nearest road was eighteen miles from his cabin. For the past five years he has lived in Canada Lake, hiking or skiing almost daily in the area covered by this guide. Stanford rechecked the routes described in this guide and discovered several new and interesting bushwhacks. When he is not outdoors, he plays the piano and studies music.